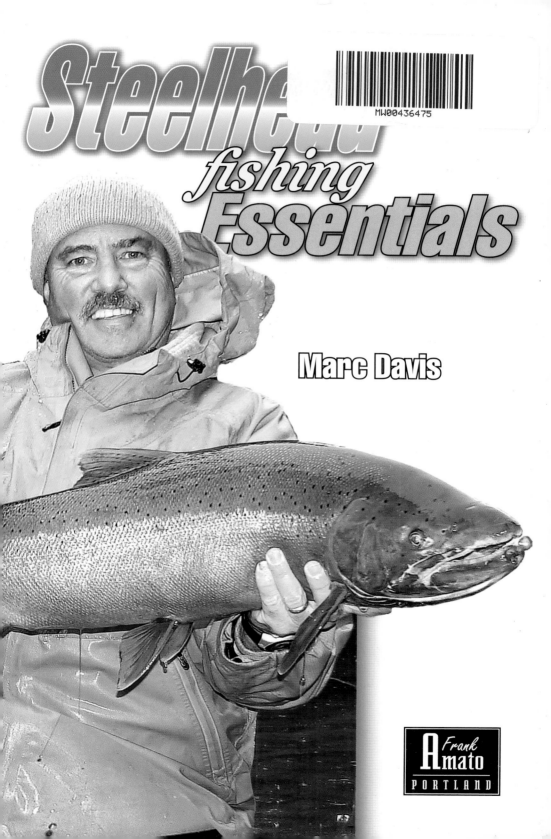

Steelhead
fishing
Essentials

Marc Davis

A *Frank* **mato**
PORTLAND

Dedication

I caught and landed my first trout on the American River in California. My dad rushed back up to the truck to get the camera. I washed the sand off the trout. The trout left. My dad didn't yell at me then or ever. My first lesson on catch-and-release came early. I sure miss him.

Acknowledgments

Here's to the sages, Paul Johnson and Walt McGovern—two of the best sounding boards a man could ever know. Thanks to my wife for keeping me on a very long leash, and a tip of the hat to the men and women who are Northwest Steelheaders. You are the ones keeping them honest!

Frank Amato Publications, Inc.
P.O. Box 82112, Portland, Oregon 97282
503.653.8108 • www.amatobooks.com

Photographs by the author unless otherwise noted.
Book Design: Kathy Johnson

Printed in Singapore
Softbound ISBN-13: 978-1-57188-450-3
UPC: 0-81127-00286-3

1 3 5 7 9 10 8 6 4 2

Table of Contents

Foreword

Steelhead fishing is a journey that many of us take as often as life, love, work, and all other things important will allow. It is a passion that drives fishers, men and women, to pursue one of the noblest creatures to swim in waters throughout the Pacific Northwest, British Columbia, Alaska, and the Great Lakes Region. One thing is well known by all who find themselves in a drift boat on a hard winter day or on the bank of a river in mid-summer when the river is low and gin clear, steelhead are elusive and even the most prepared angler with years of experience will go many trips without catching, let alone hooking a fish.

The information contained in this book and associated video provides a comprehensive overview of all aspects of steelhead angling. Everyone from the beginner to the most experienced steelhead angler will benefit from reading the information contained herein and will most certainly catch more fish. You can rest assured the author spent plenty of hours over the years perfecting every aspect of what is described in this book and is familiar with many whose job is finding ways to entice fish to bite the tackle on the end of your line.

You will not have to go far in the book to get some of the best information an steelheader can use to improve their chances of catching fish. Do a little homework in order to collect specific information on rivers you plan to fish throughout the year. Contact your local State fish and wildlife office for information on annual returns and catch statistics. You can increase your chances by knowing when and where the fish are likely to be present based on past hatchery trap counts or harvest card returns. Talk with other local anglers about the best conditions for fishing a particular river. Keep an eye on the weather and river levels several days prior to going out. The most important thing you can do is talk, talk, and then talk again to other steelhead anglers who went through many of the same pitfalls you may be experiencing on your quest.

Please remember the next time you have a beautiful steelhead dancing on the end of your line that you are squaring off with one of the most unique and diverse fish in the world. Whether it is a hatchery steelhead that you wish to have on the barbecue or a truly majestic native steelhead that deserves the utmost care when handling prior to gently releasing it back into the wild, you are experiencing something that many will unfortunately never have the opportunity to live. Enjoy the experience and learn from it in order to improve your chances the next time a steelhead bites the end of your line.

—Todd Alsbury

CHAPTER I
First Things First

This book is about the steelhead, a fish formerly thought to be a seagoing trout but now, more perfectly, called a true salmon. They are called the "fish of a thousand casts" for very good reasons. After reading this book, you may think differently.

The primary reason for steelhead fishing is catching steelhead. If you want a wonderful day in the outdoors—go on a nature hike. If you want to strike silver—do your homework. The homework is not that hard and it is much better done in a warm, wind-free, dry, well-lighted environment than out on the river.

Rule 1, Step 1, Square 1—There must be fish in the river before you can catch them! If fish aren't present, why are you getting up at a ridiculous hour, driving through fog on frosty or icy roads to catch something that isn't to be found?

There is plenty of information available on when steelhead are usually caught in your favorite river. The catch record that you must complete after keeping a fish is combined with thousands of others to compile a fine history of when fish were caught in the past on a particular river. Use this information! Some rivers begin receiving winter-run steelhead at about Thanksgiving; others don't get going until after the first of the year. Catch statistics are available for most rivers. Procure these statistics, look for the bell curve and plan your attack accordingly. Remember, however, that these catch statistics reveal the number of hatchery steelhead landed and not the number of fish in the river. If you practice catch and release rather than catch, fillet and release, you'll need more specific information available from other sources that I'll list later.

Find out at what height the river fishes best. If you normally use 15-pound main line and 12-pound leader, you will not fare well in gin-clear waters. Gather information that will guide you on the best river height to fit your method of fishing. Some rivers offer broad latitudes where they will

First light, first water and a fine piece of driftable river just below this shute, with the river all to ourselves. It doesn't get any better.

give up their treasure. Smaller streams must be within very specific parameters before there is much reason to waste the gas to visit them.

Get current information. There are tons of sources available that give you fishing reports for free or for very little cost. Printed publications are of some use but the information can be stale. Telephone or online information is probably your best, up to date source.

Contact an appropriate source and then make your decision on where ,to go based on relevant information from a reliable source.

You've done some of your homework. You know when the river contains fish in catchable numbers. You know at what level the river should be to fit your particular style of fishing, you have verified that fish are in the river and being caught—so, go already!

Where to Find Them

Steelhead are fantastic swimmers. They may spend years out in the Pacific or the Great Lakes before returning to their native waters. When they are back in their home rivers they can cover twenty miles in a day, swimming upstream. They have only two things in mind when they are in the river: staying alive and spawning.

This is where the steelheader comes in. You are in the game only to offer a brief diversion from their master plan. If you've done your homework, you know about when the fish should be in the river and about where in the river the main herd should be. You have selected your target area and you are walking down to the river bank. You got your river level information from the newspaper and now discover that it is two days stale. The river level has changed, and what was the perfect drift is either too high or too low. Now what?

The fish are probably still there and have adapted to the changed water conditions.

You can either fish or go home. If there are logs coming down the river, you might want to consider going home, but if conditions are still safe, wet a line. The current is triple what you are used to and the usual drifts are unfishable, so where are the steelhead laying? When they come into the river they have a certain amount of fuel to expend on the spawning venture. They put forth no more energy than is necessary so as to save that valuable fuel for the trip upriver and for spawning. In high-water conditions, fish will be along the side of the river in eddies and along the banks where the current is slower. That is where you must do your fishing.

The water is murky but dropping, and that's a really good sign. Fish may be caught on a rising river but they bite much better when it is stable or falling. You must use a larger drift lure to improve their ability to see your offering. The addition of some bait to add taste and smell will improve your chances of a take. Your opinion of the poor river conditions soon improves remarkably. A mint-bright steelhead took your offering and it was practically at your feet. Your next cast swings rapidly to the bank and just as you begin to reel you feel that surge from a fleeing fish. The hook is set and the fight is on. When that fish is landed you have a decision to make. You kept the first one and can tag the second. If you don't need the food, make the leap to catch-and-release fishing. You can keep fishing and that steelie with your hook still in its mouth will appreciate the gesture.

You adapted and overcame adversity. You learned two valuable lessons: get good, current information on the river, and make lemonade when life hands you lemons.

Same situation as before, but now the river is much lower and clearer than you expected. To find where the steelhead are laying you must consider the situation. They want cover because they aren't going anywhere for a while. They will look for deeper slots and holes or hang under well-oxygenated riffles that provide overhead cover. The river is too slow for a good drift so you need to fish the slots and riffles. Long, small-diameter leaders and tiny drifters with little or no bait will do the job under these conditions. Spinners might be considered if you can cast to the holding water but they, too, must be small.

The message from this chapter is to have the best and latest information on the river before you go. You must also have enough equipment to be able to adapt to changing conditions. Being able to go bigger or smaller and having the tenacity to work for those bites can turn a rotten trip into a memorable day.

Guides

You went fishing; you saw others landing fish but you weren't one of the lucky ones that got hooked up. This puts you in the category of 90% of the fishermen that go after steelhead.

If you are a golfer, I doubt you bought a bag full of clubs, wandered out on a course and shot in the upper seventies the first several times out.

Just as in any other sport, lessons are a good thing. You may ask, "Where can I get lessons on steelheading?"

Go to any serious store carrying steelhead tackle, pick up an issue of any local fishing rag or ask a friend. You will be able to locate the name of a quality guide in short order. These people are just itching to get you out on the river and put you into fish. The good part is they will probably be able to do so. The bad part is, they want money to do it.

Guides are **always** interested in building their client base. They make their best money on clients that return year after year. They **are** interested in meeting you. Going with a guide on a river that you have determined has fish

The first guide I ever used was Dave McCann. He and I go way back with lots of tales of fish from the Deschutes River and all the Tillamook Bay streams. Dave is seen here with "Frisco" Jack Dowty who is a retired river guide. The two of them are a wealth of knowledge. People ask me why I use guides so often on rivers that I know very well on my own. The simple answer is local knowledge. They were on the river years before but more importantly, they were on the river yesterday!

when you want to go will give you an education that would take years to gain going on your own. They have fished the river for years. They were fishing that river yesterday and they know where the fish live under all sorts of weather and water conditions. They know what is working now and they know what worked five years ago. They will have the proper rods, line and terminal tackle. In most instances you need only show up with a fistful of dollars, lunch, and a day to kill. The guide will take care of the rest. That day can be one of the most memorable of your life if you have done your homework. Their card, however, says "Guide," not God. They can't make fish appear out of thin air. There is a reason it's called fishing instead of catching. Get enough information to make an informed decision on which river to fish and when to fish it—**then** book a trip with the guide.

Usually, a competent guide is going to get you into fish. They like to see you succeed. They also enjoy a tip for good service. Like everyone else, guides enjoy bragging rights among their peers. I like to think of a good guide as being like an unusual Blackjack dealer that tells you when to hit and when to stand pat. They don't do their jobs for free but they are worth every penny. Standard fee for two people in a drift boat is presently about $175 a head. Say the guide has you on the river for six to eight hours. The guide also had to drive to the river so now it is eight or ten hours. Who do you think cured-up those eggs, tied all those leaders and slinkies you lost, and cleaned up the boat and truck? Now we are at ten to twelve hours. Out of that $25 to $30 an hour, they have to pay taxes, licenses, insurance, vehicle and boat expenses and usually a shuttle. Amazing how that huge guide fee came down to less than you make per hour. These folks really earn their pay. You can cooperate by landing a limit in the first quarter mile, and then everyone will go home happy—early!

Guides are required by law to be licensed and insured. Make sure your guide is just that. Look over the boat. Is there flotation gear? Is the boat clean and orderly? You don't necessarily need a neat-nut, but organization and tidiness is an indication that the guide takes his business seriously. Is the equipment in good working order? Plenty of new line, good leaders, good bait and most of the blood and egg spooge off the rod handle?

Many guides spend a lot of money advertising their services. The best, however, usually do not need to do so. Word-of-mouth is the best and cheapest advertising they can get. Ask around; someone who has had good trips with good guides will be willing to share the information.

At the beginning of the trip most guides give their clients a short talk that will set the tone for the day. They will describe the equipment and the terminal tackle. They will show you how to properly prepare your offering for quick consumption and how they like to "do it." Listen up! Remember, he's on your side. You're paying this person to get you into fish but also to show you how they get you into fish. Keep your eyes open. Watch what other people are doing in

other boats that are catching fish. Keep an eye on hook size, leader length, terminal tackle and where both they and you are catching fish. Mentally record that information and keep a journal. Mine is thirty years old and has vital information about every trip (more on this later). Watch the surface of the water and imagine what's going on beneath it. Learning to read water is one of the most valuable lessons. If you stay awake you will learn much faster. Ask questions! Lots of 'em! Most guides can row and talk at the same time. They are glad to share most information. Best not to ask what's in the egg cure, however.

Steelhead have a bad habit of waiting until the warm morning sun has lulled you to sleep before they send that tender twitch up your line. The light slowly comes on and you wonder, "Was that a bite?" Too late! It was, and you missed it. Show up ready to play the game by getting some sleep the night before. The guide can get you to fish but you have to do the rest. "Whiffed" hook-sets or, worse yet, broken leaders can send the wrong message: that you aren't really serious about this and you don't have your head in the game. You and your guide are a team. If you aren't going to keep your eye on the ball, the guide will figure this out and your trip could turn into a boat ride.

Show up for the trip on time and ready to rumble. A good guide will help you with the rest.

Money

Steelheaders, golfers and duck hunters are some of the craziest people I know. Who in their right mind would want to get up at "0 dark thirty" to drive on slippery roads and spend the day in a frosty aluminum boat, or stand butt deep in icy water to catch a steelhead that they'll probably throw back anyway? The answer is you. True believers involved in the three religions mentioned above will make any sacrifice to further their knowledge of the sport.

Left: Professional guide Chris Vertopoulos on the river with two really happy clients.

But what if you're not that gung-ho yet? You're just beginning and can't quite see your way clear to purchase that $329 Loomiwick boron rod with Kryptonite-lined guides. The reel to go with that rod will easily bring it up to half a grand. What's a person to do?

By doing a little homework, you can put together a great rod and reel combination for less than a hundred bucks, including the line. A set of boots and good rain gear will be about another hundred. Add a vest and a selection of terminal tackle and you have spent the price of a mediocre putter. This will get you on the river and give you the equipment needed to cause trouble for our migrating quarry. How do you find the right equipment? That guide we mentioned in the last chapter would be a good start. Sales people may not be the best sources for information; they're likely to sell you what they have the most of. Other steelheaders, however, are an excellent source of information. They will be grouped into three main camps: fly-fishers, level-winders and spinning rodders. For beginners, I suggest starting with spinning gear. It is inexpensive, easily mastered, and can catch fish with the

Steelhead never give up. They fight you tooth and nail to the boat or bank. Just when you think they're bested—a flip and they're gone! Steelies would make good Marines.

Way back when I had dark hair I kept this lovely lady to put on my wall. She was landed on the Queets River on the Olympic Peninsula in Washington. The skin mount cost $400 back then and still looks great many years later. Now she would have been measured for length and girth, photographed closely and released to be replaced by a fiberglass replica.

best of them. Good spinning reels can be purchased at discount stores for less than $30. The line to fill that reel will run you another $10, and a suitable quality rod is available for less than $50. As of this writing, I have landed fifteen steelhead over twenty pounds. Thirteen of those fish were landed on a noodle rod and spinning reel combination, with the other two coming off a level-wind. Only nine of them were landed from the bank, however. Start with a spinning rod and then move on to the other methods after you've mastered the basics. None of my noodle rods cost over fifty dollars and the reels were about sixty. Find a rod-and-reel combo that feels good in your hands and use it.

CHAPTER II

Tackle and Bait

Line

Hooks and line are the two most important parts of this equation. If the jerk on one end doesn't set the hook in the jerk on the other end—nothing happens. The line must fit the type of fishing you choose to do. If it is too heavy, the fish will be discouraged from biting or won't hold on to the bait. If the line is too light, you'll probably lose the fish in the fight, if the leader even survives the hook set. Eight- to fifteen-pound-test main line is standard for most successful fishermen. For the last fifteen years, I have used nothing but eight- or ten-pound test for both line and leader. This is quite light and forces me to relinquish a lot of tackle that could have been salvaged had I used a heavier line. By using a light spinning rod I am able to avoid breaking line on the hook-set, but I can't turn bigger fish that decide to head downstream. I lose a few fish in the fight but I feel I hook a lot more fish because of the lighter line. I do not like lines that glow; if you need those lines to fish, you might consider stronger glasses. Fish that have just come in from the ocean are not at all leader or line shy. Those that have been exposed to a few hundred drifted offerings tend to be more wary. If you must use high-visibility lines, you might think about fishing closer to big water. I have found lines that match the water color will usually get me into more fish. The lower the visibility of the line and more importantly, the leader, the higher the likelihood the fish will bite even after being pounded on a heavily fished river. Monofilament lines that have provided the best service for me over the years are Maxima, Stren and Ande. These lines have good color characteristics, resistance to abrasion, knot strength and are moderately low in cost. Almost weekly there are new lines and leaders appearing on the market. Buy a leader pack and try them out. That's how we find out about new things that really work.

Spending a few cents more per leader will get you into the stuff that is completely limp and virtually disappears in the water. The two best leader materials I have come

Robert Bradley from Oregon Dept. of Fish and Wildlife has helped "build" millions of salmon and steelhead. This is his largest hatchery steelie taken on the Wilson River on drift gear.

across are Izorline and Segar. These two have excellent knot strength, very small diameter, low stretch, and are nearly invisible. It is not necessary to spend big bucks on the line but stealthy leaders are a must if you're fishing high-traffic areas.

Kevlar or Spectra lines have properties all their own that can be good once you get used to them. They have no stretch at all, so it's easy to break fish off with vigorous hook-sets and even easier to break a rod on a snag. They float like a fly line and their diameter is unbelievably small for the line test. These lines will transmit every nuance of the bottom to the rod, but can cut a finger like a band-saw blade. They require special knots to work properly for very long and I've found that a small drop of superglue on the dry line will make the knots last forever. I have been using these lines for about five years and have yet to replace any of them.

The one I use most for bobbers was getting a little bleached out so I just turned it around on the reel and expect to get another five years service. The lines are completely limp, so backlashes are best avoided if possible because the knots can be troublesome to get loose. For bobber-fishing and plug-trolling, 30-pound-test Toughline Plus is hard to beat. These lines work equally well on both level-wind and spinning reels.

Hooks

Hooks are not a good place to save money. Since the hook is the pointy end of the spear in this battle, you want to make sure it has a good tip. Very few hooks are sharp right out of the package. There are some exceptions, but you'll generally pay more for a sharp point fresh out of the box. The best hooks I've found for fishing in rocky areas are Owner Super Needle Point hooks or VMC's. They will take rock hits and still keep fishing, and take several sharpenings before needing replacement. For drift fishing in less snaggy areas, I prefer the Owner Cutting Point hook. The points are incredibly sharp and they have increased my number of hookups substantially while standing up to hard-fighting fish without breakage. Regardless of your hook brand, you can't go wrong with a Luhr Jensen hook file kept safely (and rust-free) in a file protector loaded with WD-40. These inexpensive devices are available at most tackle shops and pay for themselves in files that will last for years.

Lead

Pencil lead is one of the most popular methods of getting your offering down to the zone where fish live. It is inexpensive to buy and very effective to use. There are many methods of attaching your weight to the line, and the KISS Principle applies (keep it simple, stupid). Lead will be lost frequently. If you aren't losing gear you aren't fishing. 'Elegant' and 'ornate' are not words that need to be used with lead. If I could figure out a good way of using rocks instead of lead I would do so. On a bad day I might go through two dozen rigs on a snaggy river. Time spent

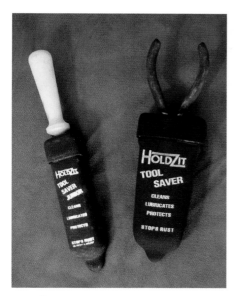

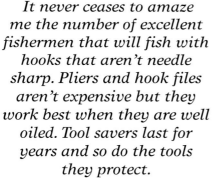

It never ceases to amaze me the number of excellent fishermen that will fish with hooks that aren't needle sharp. Pliers and hook files aren't expensive but they work best when they are well oiled. Tool savers last for years and so do the tools they protect.

No matter what, you will need weight to get down to the fish. Most steelhead streams are laden with snags so you are going to lose gear. Of the three, lead is the most prone to getting hung up but it is quickly replaced. Slinkies and sinkies make excellent scent carriers and are almost snag free in rocky areas. By using the Sinkie you get the bottom feel of lead and fewer snags while retaining the benefit of a better scent-disbursing tool.

out of the water re-rigging a complicated lead is time when the bait is not in front of a steelie's nose. Homework applies especially to lead. Anything you can do at the kitchen table means more time spent with your offering in the water. Complicated lead rigs should never be manufactured on the river but in a warm, dry, well-lit environment.

The most popular method of building slinkies is to use parachute shroud filled with lead shot. A commercial

Lead Rig

To Rod

To Terminal Gear

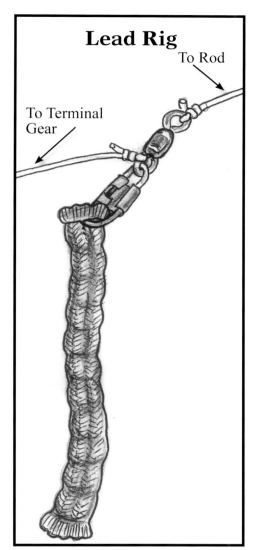

slinkie-building tool makes this process much quicker, as the shot is tough to get into the tube without one. To make slinkies, simply place the shot in the tube and cut it, leaving about a quarter inch of nylon. Expose the nylon to a candle's heat and lightly crimp the melted end with a pair of needle-nosed pliers. To attach the slinkie to the line just open a small black snap swivel and place it through the slinkie fabric. This can go on the line as a solid tie or as a slip rig.

A little later in the book we will explore weights and how your sinker can be used to dramatically increase the number of steelhead that will wind up on your hook!

Catching steelhead is all about time spent with your gear in the water. You must be comfortable with what you use and it has to give the right presentation to the fish to be effective. Your choice of a "sinker" system is as important as your choice of bait.

Left: This tailout is a place where a well-situated plug could cause a lot of commotion in a big hurry. Few things in life cause larger surges of adrenalin than a Hotshot bite! Learning to read water well dramatically reduces the time between bites.

CHAPTER III

At the End of the Line

Terminal Tackle and Baits

Ever watch a baby that discovers a bauble? When they see something new it goes right into the mouth. Steelhead are no different except they don't have fingers. When they see something that interests them they have only one means of testing and that's tasting. Usually they will see your offering first. They will approach for a closer inspection and then inhale it. This is the same whether the bait is a fly, gob of eggs, spoon or a corkie. Once it's in the mouth the fish will quickly decide whether to hold or reject the bait. It is that split second of hesitation that causes so many fish to wind up on the bank. **Anything** you can do to prolong the take will dramatically increase your chances of hooking the fish. Bait is often effective not only because it smells good, but is usually soft and tastes good too. The fish will hold on long enough for the line to tighten and the strike to be felt. Then the fun begins.

Natural baits come in many forms and colors. Most mimic something steelhead eat in the wild. Eggs, shrimp, sand shrimp, even nightcrawlers are all excellent baits that prolong the take to the point the bait is swallowed. This is a good thing if you intend to kill the fish, but not so good if you intend to release it. A deeply hooked fish is much more likely to be hooked in the gills or even a vital organ that is adjacent to the gullet. Keep this in mind when selecting your bait. Native fish are too valuable to risk deep hooking. Hatchery fish were designed to be taken home.

Roe is one of the most popular baits because it is fairly available and found to be quite acceptable to steelhead under the right conditions. Roe can be cured in a variety of ways and many of them are effective. In general, you want roe to retain its "eggy" look; you do not want the eggs to lose their roundness. When the eggs hit the water they should "milk" out. The most often used colors for eggs are red, hot

pink and their natural orange. Nearly all steelheaders have a favorite egg cure and most would rather part with their wallet in a mugging than give up their secret cure, even to their closest friend. That doesn't prevent the friend from attempting to find the recipe by bribing children, hiding video cameras or home invasion at gunpoint. A good egg cure is worth more than its weight in gold. That will be topic for discussion at length later in the book.

Sand Shrimp

These critters are expensive and delicate. They must be selected with care and kept in an appropriate environment or they quickly become catfish bait. A refrigerator that is not too cold will assist these crustaceans in adding one or two days to their lives. Your life will be sweeter (and longer) if you do not manage to let them get loose in the fridge. Your spouse will assure you that sand shrimp and Jell-O do not go together under any circumstances. Even if the shrimp are kept in a stable temperature they will still quickly degrade due to their urine. In the store container the big boys will crawl to the top and pee on the smaller

On days when I am unable to get fresh sand shrimp or if there are a lot of folks on the water I will go to my preserved shrimp. I always seem to have plenty of left-over shrimp and at the end of the day I'll boil them in a brine with a preservative. Sometimes I'll use a dye to give them a little added color. These shrimp were dyed dipping one end in radiant green Bad Azz dye and the other end in red by the same manufacturer. They will last for months in a fridge or freezer and will definitely give you the edge when fishing with crowds or in murky water.

ones below. This results in a few live lobster-size shrimp and a bunch of smelly, smaller dead ones on the bottom. To cure this problem the shrimp should be placed in a flat container with only one layer of shrimp spaced well apart. There should be a "diaper" under the shrimp, several layers of paper towels will work nicely. Fresh shrimp can be kept for several days in a cooler if the diapers are changed daily.

Shrimp do not react well to sunlight or rain. An open container of costly shrimp will quickly go downhill if left unprotected in the sun or rain. Take care of this bait and it will serve you well for several days.

Drifted shrimp can be a deadly bait. "Fresh-in" steelies will inhale them like candy. Fish that have been in the river for awhile will take them readily, and even spawned-out fish will jump on a good shrimp. Many anglers use a whole shrimp either behind a drift lure or by itself. Due to the soft nature of the shrimp's body they usually do not stay on the hook for many casts. If you use a whole shrimp, make sure you break off the big claw on the larger males. The claw can really get in the way of a hook's point. I prefer to use only the tail, either by itself or behind a drifter.

Drift Lures

Some of the more popular drift lures are Spin N Glos and corkies. These come in most every size and color imaginable. For some reason that no one seems to understand, fish are very selective about the size and color of an offering. A particular color may be just the thing one year. You go out and buy them on sale by the hundreds and then the fish refuse them the next season. Fish will also switch color

A lovely winter steelie taken at the head of a drift in mid-winter on a corkie laced with scent.

and/or size preference during the day, to stay up with the bite one must have a selection of drifters to match the changing preference of the fish.

A general rule seems to apply: Use drifters with bigger silhouettes under murky water conditions and smaller cross sections under clear water conditions. Use bright colors in bright or sunny conditions and muted col-

A lovely winter steelie taken at the head of a drift in mid-winter on a corkie laced with scent.

ors when it's cloudy, rainy or darkening. Most steelheaders would say that if they had to have only one drifter in their vest it would be a medium to small pink pearl. Fish that are lower in the rivers are more likely to bite on larger drifters. Exposure to possibly hundreds of rigs down lower in the river makes them wary biters by the time they get well into the watershed. If fish seem to be a little shy to bite, try going to a smaller, more subtle offering without bait.

By the time a fish has survived long enough to reach the upper river, it has had the opportunity to see and hit a multitude of lures and baits. Drifter size also has a rule appropriate to the river section: On the lower coastal rivers where fish are fresh in from the salt, use larger drifters, bigger hooks and more yarn. Once the critters have been exposed to a number of drifted baits, it's best to go to smaller leaders, smaller drifters and smaller hooks with little or no yarn. Bigger drifters and bigger hooks mean more hookups and fish landed in the lower rivers. Smaller offerings mean more hits, but you pay the price in fish landed due to smaller hook size and more broken leaders.

Fishing in the Dark

Some states allow fishing for steelhead and salmon all night on certain waters, while others are more restrictive. Oregon allows us to begin one hour before sunrise and we must stop one hour after sunset in most instances. Over 30 years ago I discovered glow-in-the-dark corkies and I began using them for my first few casts in the morning. Usually the best time of day on our Northwest streams is first light or just after for steelhead. Often I found that the fish were not laying in their usual spots but were much closer to shore or in shallower water than when the light was brighter. I began using luminous drifters earlier in the day, right at legal time in the morning. After I learned where they would

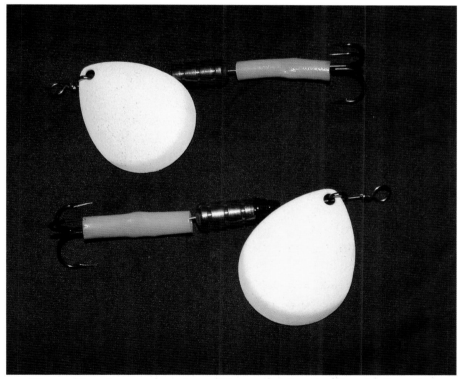

If you live in a state that allows fishing in the dark or in low light periods you are missing a great bet if you don't use phosphorescent lures. Fish are the least spooked during low or no light and get really upset when something pushes them out of their selected territory for the evening.

*Glow-in-the-dark drifters are on the end of my noodle rod
about 98% of the time. Steelhead see things a lot differently
than humans and I have found that "glowies" make a huge
difference in the number of hookups I get even in clear water.
In low light or poor visibility situations they are a must.
In clear water I switch to a smaller size.*

be in darkness, I began catching most of my fish while the
stars were still out. This opened up a whole new aspect
to fishing and my lifestyle changed. I transferred jobs to
be near the rivers and I would go fishing before heading
for work. This was in the good ol' days when there were
still lots of summer steelhead hatchery fish and plenty of
winter clipped-fins still available. I'd get a limit and fillet
the fish streamside then remove the carcass for deposition
in the office dumpster. The fillets were placed in the office
lunchroom refrigerator. The one not-so-small problem I had
to overcome was the definite odor of fish on my hands. This

was taken care of with a bottle of lemon juice kept just for hand cleaning. Several of the ladies complained that there were fish parts proximal to their Tupperware but occasional gifts of extremely fresh steelhead fillets quieted that objection in a hurry and we continued to exist in harmony.

I figured out that if the behavior of fish in the morning was totally different maybe it was the same in the evening. Some of the best fishing of my life occurred on those summer and fall evenings after work. The later in the day the better the fishing, and it was phenomenal just at legal quitting time with fish often right at my feet. As summer melded into fall I was joined by hunters who were interested in the light in the woods down by the river and I got to know several of the game enforcement officers. I wore one of the Casio alarm watches and showed them it was set to go off five minutes before legal time, they would honk but never bother to stop if they saw my vehicle after that.

Sand shrimp became available in local stores about that time and the number of fish landed was easily doubled using a small portion of these critters with the glow-in-the-dark corkies. It was during this time that I developed the low-rodding technique. I was often fishing in total darkness and everything was by feel. Back then we landed fish with a net and you learned to scoop about a foot behind the lighted corkie for best results and a fish in the net. One of my photographer friends began using another new item, an electronic photo flash. Those things really lit up the drifters but if any light got on the water or reflected on the brush fish would scatter immediately. A small flashlight with a halogen bulb seemed to be a better weapon of choice and it was good for getting in and out of the hole. I think the very bright drifter going through the black velvet of the hole was sometimes a little too much for the fish. The flashlight provided a more subtle and attractive lure.

Steelhead, like many other critters, have vision far different from our own. Their vision is oriented to the particular portion of the light spectrum that allows them to best forage for their food in open sea and rivers. To survive they must evade both finny and avian predators and need specifically geared to do it. I have found that using luminescent drifters even in full daylight encourages bites from fish that might not have otherwise been interested. The people I fish with will usually be fishing with about the same gear. If I'm using phosphorescent drifters while they are using only fluorescent lures there are usually more fish landed on the rod in my hand. One color combination is my favorite, day in and day out: a reddish pink and white corkie covered with fluorescent (glow in the dark) overcoating. I call it the Candy Cane and it is a top producer. Right behind it is another hot-pink corkie without the luminous paint, partially covered with just a hint of iridescent purple scale. I'm not sure why steelies find these two so attractive, I'm just sure that they do. If I had to fish for the rest of my life using only one or two drifters it would be these two in size 10 or 12.

Fishing from the bank using luminous drifters presents some problems that can be overcome with a little preparation. Using spinning gear is a big plus because it's less prone to tangling or backlashes. It's best to begin your morning or evening adventure with lures attached and spares already fully tied and in your pocket or vest. That way only one knot is needed when you need to retie. A second fully rigged rod is a must. If your rig gets really screwed up in the dark it will happen when the bite is hottest and about to end due to daylight or the end of legal fishing time.

Over the years I have stopped using bait for steelhead at night because I don't need it; they bite really well on a good scent and I don't have to worry about them swallowing it.

This last season I kept only two fish for the table and I had zero fish in any distress. All were mouth hooked and released.

If you are going to try this method, an excellent purchase would be an LED headlamp to show you where the rocks and holes are along the river. It also keeps your hands free for carrying and balance. A small halogen flashlight is a big plus. Approach the water in stealth mode and make no unnecessary noise in the water. When you hook a fish and are landing it try to move the fish out of the lie so it does not disturb the others that may be close by. If you know there are fish out in front of you try catching downstream fish first. Just like turkey hunters of old used to do, shoot the one on the back of the string and work your way up to the front.

Steelies tend to be much more aggressive on takes in the dark and fishing with luminous spoons or spinners can be a real blast. Many hits will happen just as you lift the lure out of the water and, in the dark, that's a real cage rattler.

It's easy to make most any lure phosphorescent with brush-on paint; most spoons and spinners are easily coated with the glow material. Some of the best paint comes from magic shops rather than tackle providers. Clean the lures well and lightly buff them with 000 steel wool. Put several coats of paint on even an old crusty lure and it can turn into a real killer.

Winter fish seem to respond well to larger drifters up to a size-eight corkie, but summer fish seem to like the smaller presentations in size ten or twelve. Get up earlier and begin fishing at legal time for these steelies and you won't be disappointed.

An additional advantage of fishing in reduced or no light is that you will gain a better feel for everything you do on the river: Your ability to detect bites by feel will dramatically improve and your ability to deftly tie knots will become that of a surgeon. All of the above will add to your tally of fish on the bank.

Yarn Applications

To use or not to use? Yarn increases the silhouette and allows a mixture of colors in your bait. It also allows for a better disbursement of scent if you decide to use one. Most importantly, it tends to catch in the fish's teeth and allows just a little more time to set the hook. If you use yarn, I recommend using a contrasting color opposite from the drifter. There is no reason to use only one color of yarn. Yarn (or wool as our neighbors to the North call it) comes in many forms: Plain knitting yarn lies straight behind

*Norm Richie and professional guide Erik Brigham on the
Lewis River in Washington. A tad of yarn and a few eggs
side drifting got this one invited home for dinner.*

the hook in fast or slow water. "Fuzzy" yarn fluffs out in
slow water and lays back in faster water to give the bait
a pulsating action. The yarn should never be long enough
to interfere with the bite by covering the hook point. Yarn
can be added to the hook by slipping it through the loop
(if you are using an egg loop), tying it on the line above the
hook with an overhand knot or integrated into the egg loop

Ear Plug Bugs are some of my favorite drifters. They have the buggy nature of a fly but retain the soft body of eggs. If you properly bevel the front of the foam they have a slight wiggle in the current and the closed foam holds scent for long periods.

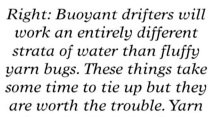

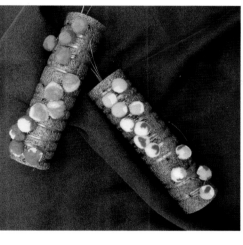

Right: Buoyant drifters will work an entirely different strata of water than fluffy yarn bugs. These things take some time to tie up but they are worth the trouble. Yarn is an excellent carrier for scent and the fish will hang on to them a split second longer than a hard-bodied drifter.

when the hook is being tied. Tying yarn into the loop allows for using the loop but not for easily changing yarn colors.

The Doublecross

Most of my coastal river fish and five of my largest steelhead were caught on a Doublecross. This drift lure retains the round, eggy silhouette of a corkie but gives the lure a decidedly "buggy" appearance that drives steelies nuts. The most effective color combination is a flame or rocket red corkie combined with white yarn. Other color combos work but this one seems to have a special appeal. The sideburns on the Doublecross work best if there is just enough yarn to allow for pulsation in current but not so much that the roundness of the drifter is hidden. This lure is easily made using all sizes of corkies, but I prefer size 10 or 12 with a number 1 or 1/0 hook. Bait below a Doublecross seems to be unnecessary; they work quite well on their own without anything on the hook. Experimentation is key to this lure. Try adding a little bit of Flashabou to the yarn or mixing yarn colors. You will find a combo you like and, more importantly, that fish like.

See the DVD on how to build your own Doublecross rigs.

The Doublecross is my "go to" rig for coastal rivers. I don't know what it is about the drifter but it looks "buggy" in the water with the undulations of the sideburns. It floats a lot higher than a rag but it has all the possible color combinations that fishermen and fish seem to prefer.

Winter steelhead landed on the Wilson River using orange corkies with white yarn to make the Doublecross.

Another limit of steelhead that succumbed to the Doublecross.

*Late-winter steelhead landed
on Oregon's Wilson River
using the Doublecross
and scent.*

*Handle fish gently, like you
would a human baby, and
let them go to make babies
of their own.*

The Rag

Another lure with a "buggy" appearance is the rag. Made with a short length of round foam and yarn the rag can carry your color fancies as far as you want to take them.

They are cheap, easily made, and very effective, especially in higher water. This is another lure that does not need bait added to be effective

The Rag

Spinners

These lures produce even more vicious strikes than a spoon. When steelies hit spinners they seem to be really aggressive and irritated. They don't want to just eat the lure but kill it—twice.

Spinners usually won't sink as fast on the retrieve as a spoon. They won't cast as far either. Spoons can be cast 60 or 70 yards, while a spinner of equal weight will only make it about 30. Think of a spoon as a long rifle needing a scope and a weighted spinner as a 45 pistol for up-close work. Each has their optimal arena. Spoons are usually gaudy and flashy while spinners are either shiny or dull and muted. Darker days or cloudy water usually call for darker-bodied spinners while bright sun or cloudless skies call for something with flash. Spinners work best if kept below the boundary layer (see the illustration on page 40). Spinners should not be used with a snap swivel or even a snap. The spinning blade acts as a shield to protect the line from direct hits with rocks or snags. Lure speed and size need to reflect the water in which you are fishing. Deep, fast water needs a heavier lure, while slow drifts can use something lighter that will sink more slowly.

Casting perpendicular to the stream's flow works best with spinners. Let them sink to the boundary layer and then retrieve. Casts parallel to the shore often yield results but snags are more likely. If you are really brave, try upstream casts. Let the lure sink near bottom and then retrieve quickly. Upstream hits are eye-openers for both you and the fish; there's no doubt about what just happened.

Both spinners and spoons are expensive. Always set the hook on a stop. Often steelies grab either lure and just stop, failure to immediately set the hook will result in lost fish that should have hit the bank. Many of your stops, however, will be on rocks or sticks. If you didn't bury the barb in the snag it can usually be recovered. First: **don't jerk!** This will only set the hook deeper into the snag. Get above the snag and let out about eight to ten yards of line. This will form a belly below the snag. When the line pulls tight, give the rod a very sharp snap. Repeat several times. This should pull the lure downstream from the snag and free it. If this doesn't work, point the rod at the snag, reel in and pull the line. This may pull the lure free by straightening the hook or pulling the snag free of the bottom. If it doesn't work, you'll see why this can be an expensive way to fish.

When fishing either spinners or spoons, you will encounter more biters if the lure is kept in the water below the boundary layer. In deep runs the layer may be quite thick, but in shallower water, the layer is only inches thin. Turbulence is created as the water encounters structure along the bottom. This turbulence provides fish the

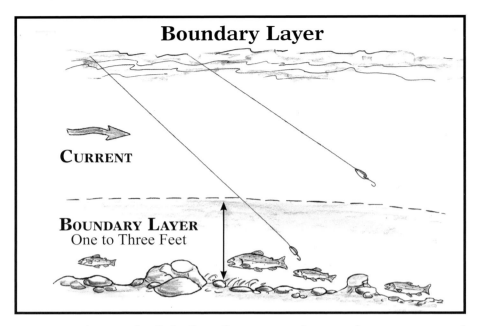

Boundary Layer

CURRENT

BOUNDARY LAYER
One to Three Feet

opportunity to duck below faster-moving surface water and rest. Once they become comfortable they are reluctant to move unless frightened or provoked. A spinner or spoon going by overhead poses little or no threat. A lure coming by at eye level needs to be dealt with, however, and a slashing strike is probable.

The depth of the boundary layer changes with water depth and speed. Its depth may be determined by the subtle change in the action of a spoon or spinner being retrieved. As the lure approaches bottom it will drop into the layer and the pull will lessen. This is where you want the lure to be. It is in the zone where it causes maximum consternation to the steelhead being approached; it's moving more slowly and is easily grabbed. It is also in the snag zone, so care must be taken to keep the lure off the bottom. Fishing the boundary layer can be expensive until the technique is mastered, but the rewards are worth the investment in tackle.

Bobbers and Sideplaners

Both steelhead and salmon have a sixth sense that allows them to remove a bobber from sight when you are not looking. Cast after cast you can stare a hole through a bobber for maybe two hours. Let something distract your attention for two seconds and the bobber is gone. A bobber down is not a bad thing but a bobber coming back up after a fish has let go is a tragedy.

Fishing with a bobber demands some degree of concentration and dedication. There are places that are so snaggy that the only alternative is to run a bobber through them or pay the price with loss of drift gear or spinners. The bobber keeps the bait in the strike zone and above the tackle grabbers. Proper use of a bobber gives a very natural float through a drift and allows the offering to remain in the slot for tens of yards. Only fishing from a boat or using a sideplaner will give a longer shot at fish in the slot.

There are hundreds of different styles of floats and bobbers. The bobbers on page 44 are examples of more frequently used models. The two most common methods of rigging are fixed depth and slider or slip rigged. With a fixed rig the distance between the bait and float does not change. As long as the depth is not extreme the fixed method works well. If a longer cast is necessary or the drift is fairly deep (six feet or more) the slip method will probably work better. A hookset on a fixed rig requires moving the bobber, lead and bait before the line tightens on the hook. With a slip rig, tension is delivered directly to the hook.

Virtually anything that can be used for drift fishing can be used under a bobber. Some of the more popular baits are jigs, eggs, worms and shrimp. If a jig is used alone the float must be small and the jig fairly large. The jig must sink fast enough to get down in the drift and have sufficient weight to set the float. To use a lighter jig and still have the float in position, lead may be attached above the jig and below the float. This same process may be used with bait. Most baits do not have sufficient weight and need lead to get them to the strike zone.

I have seen many people use feather-and-yarn jigs under a bobber but only recently began using this rig personally. Many of the places I fish for steelhead have a bottom covered with rocks the size of bowling balls. Throw in a

Bobber Rigs

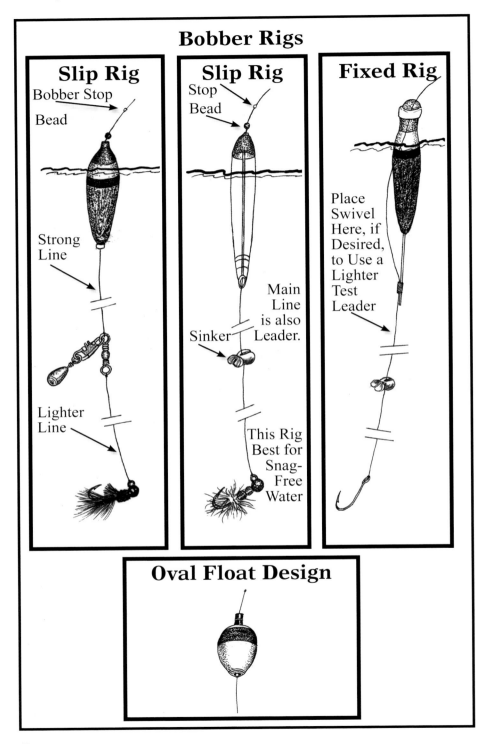

Slip Rig

Bobber Stop

Bead

Strong Line

Lighter Line

Slip Rig

Stop
Bead

Main Line is also Leader.

Sinker

This Rig Best for Snag-Free Water

Fixed Rig

Place Swivel Here, if Desired, to Use a Lighter Test Leader

Oval Float Design

little wood and we have the ideal situation for losing lots of gear. I was always told that if you aren't getting hung up you aren't fishing. That truism has validity until you begin fishing with a bobber and jig. The equipment is pretty much standard steelhead gear with a longer rod and spinning reel. A Kevlar line improves the handling of the whole thing by keeping the line on top of the water, thereby making it easier to set the hook. The bobber needs to be easily cast and one that goes down with a minimum of pull.

A bobber takedown by a steelie in fast water bears absolutely no resemblance to the slow suck of a big chinook in tidewater. The bobber is bouncing along through the riffles, dancing in and out of sight as it splashes playfully through the ripples. You are watching it intently (you think) until the light comes on and a portion of your brain tells you the bobber is underwater and heading upstream. That longer rod I spoke of comes into play here and takes care of the line you failed to mend just before the hit occurred. The beauty of bobber and jig hits is that the hook is nearly always neatly imbedded in the upper jaw and the fish will usually be landed because of this hook orientation.

Since the days when man hung out in caves, humans have enjoyed making their own weapons. Fly-fishers take pleasure in tying their secret pattern. With drift fishermen a corkie, is a corkie is a corkie. It's hard to get too technical unless you get into yarn bugs and Flashabou thingies without a name. With jigs, however, we have the opportunity to enjoy the best of both worlds. Feathers, glue, thread, head cement, yarn and hooks come together in infinite patterns that delight fishermen and sometimes even fool the fish. There is huge satisfaction in designing, making and using a successful jig pattern that will allow repeated trips through that infernal snag hole that you know always holds a fish or two. Whether you build your own spear, load your own shells or tie your own jigs you will experience the same satisfaction when you set the hook on that first "homemade jig" steelie.

A poor man's drift boat is the definition of a sideplaner. This device has been around for years and has proven

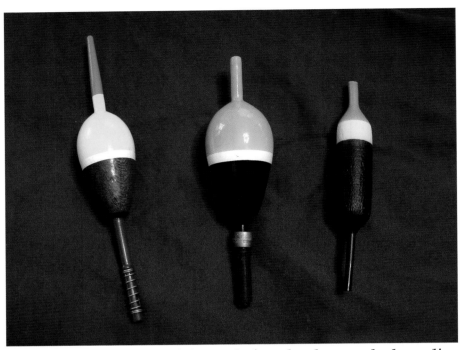

The two bobbers on the left are designed to be attached to a line and are "fixed" floats. The bobber on the right is designed to have the line move through its center and move up and down the line necessitating a bobber stop knot be used to set the depth of the jig or bait.

very effective at keeping both lures and bait in the slot. At first the sideplaner appears complicated but after several launches the operation is mastered and the true fishing begins. Sideplaners allow the fisherman to keep bait in a slot for hours or to roam up and down an open bank hitting slots both near and far. In only a few minutes the operator will learn how to guide the planer to any portion of the river that is within reach. They are not expensive and can actually be a lot of fun to drive with a little practice. They can be operated in a static mode where the lure waits for passing fish or actively propelled to different locations in search of a waiting biter.

There are few shy nibbles on sideplaners. A quick thud and a jumping fish is the usual routine, followed by an adrenaline

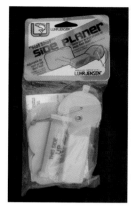 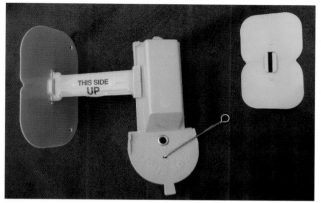

When I first used a sideplaner I thought it was a lot of hard work and that it was a silly contraption. A good friend showed me how they really work and now I love to play with them. If there are no other people around to interfere with your mobility you can quickly learn how to maneuver a sideplaner clear across a medium sized river and put a plug dead center onto the fish. When I fish the Nushagak River in Alaska I take my biggest fish using a modified sideplaner and a large pink plug with the trebles removed and a 6/0 siwash hook on the business end. The rod goes into the rod holder and I read a book until the rod folds over. Big salmon love these things and what gets towed behind them. They are the ultimate stealth weapon for steelies. The salmon never know you're there until it's too late!

rush on the part of the fisherman. The easiest way to learn how to use one is to follow the directions that come with the package, there are a lot of gimmicks on the market that don't work as promised, this is not one of them. Used in an open expanse of water with no other fishermen nearby, this device works exceptionally well.

When you get a hit on the sideplaner set the hook twice. The initial hookset clears the sideplaner on the line and releases it to slide. The second hookset drives the barbs home and keeps the fish attached.

On a larger river the right rod and line must be used to effectively work the sideplaner. The rod must have enough backbone to successfully set the hook at a good distance. It must also be long enough to hold the line off the water when the sideplaner is at longer distances from the fisherman. A longer rod makes for easy launching out into the current. The line needs to be small diameter, have little stretch and must float. Spectra lines work well in all three categories. The sideplaner does not have to be used on big rivers. By its nature it allows a fisherman to explore the far bank on smaller streams without alerting spooky fish that a threat is close by. In these places a spinner or spoon will usually work well but the sideplaner allows one to keep the lure in their faces for a long period, to the point where fight or flight is the only option.

Plugs

A relatively new technique is back-trolling plugs. Someone, probably a displaced bass fisherman, got the bright idea of tossing a plug at a steelhead and was obviously pleased with what happened. Pulling a plug through a slot or tailout can result in truly vicious strikes. Plugs are let out behind the boat above the area to be fished. The boat is pointed upstream and propelled slower than the current causing the boat and lures to proceed slowly downstream. This presents the plugs to fish established on their lie. The territorial nature of steelhead precludes invasion and once their space has been violated—look out!

On the upper Clackamas River in Oregon I have had the opportunity to watch hundreds of steelhead approached by plugs. They begin to get agitated when they can hear the lure, well before it is in sight. As the lure gets within viewing distance they usually treat it very respectfully by moving around side to side. They will then drop back a little as though the plug is pushing them from their hold. When they have had enough of the invasion they either shoot around the plug and head upstream or square off with the lure and charge. This is why the strikes are so vicious. The critters have murder in their heart when they smack the lure. One of the reasons that it's so important to have all the plugs at the same distance from the boat is to thwart the steelies that decide to flee. They are routed by one plug and decide to go around the boat after being pushed downstream. Just when they are good and irritated by one plug they have managed to avoid, there's another one right in their face. It's too much; they will dispatch this noisy little violator and get back to resting. It is about this time that one of the fishermen gets a sudden awakening with a folded rod and screaming drag.

Don't Touch That Rod!

The fish has something in its mouth that would be akin to you biting down on a hedgehog. They are trying to get rid of it with flared gills, open mouth and a shaking head. An overzealous hookset at this point simply rips it from their open mouths. After about 2/10 of a second they realize they are hooked and usually flee away from the boat. A lift on the rod now firmly imbeds the hooks in the corner of the jaw. Setting the hook any earlier is sure to snatch defeat from the jaws of victory.

Plug Selection

Some general rules for plugs are that the lower and clearer the water, the smaller the plug should be. Too much plug will cause too few strikes as the steelie will be intimidated rather than irritated. Bright days call for glittery plugs with flash and darker days work best with more muted colors. Stained or muddy waters yield more fish with darker plugs having a good silhouette and a rattle that causes a charge because the invader is so close. A chrome body with black back, chrome body with glow orange back, green and blue pirate, cop car, copper and flame orange plugs in your favorite styles will give you a good supply of trouble makers. A simple way to make sure all plugs will be behind the boat the same distance is to string the lures out with the boat at anchor. All lures are let out the same distance at the same time. When at the right distance they are stopped and a bobber stop knot is securely tied at the first guide on the rod. This knot will assure a beautiful alignment for future attacks. If more distance is required, align the knots below the rods at the same distance. Foolproof, isn't it?

Many of these lures are for bass unless they are specifically made for salmon and steelhead. It's a good idea to replace the hooks with ones that are big enough to hang on to the jaw of an ocean-burnished chromer at twenty miles an hour. If the hooks are too close to the body, add an oval slip ring or even a swivel to give a little space. That space is the necessary gap to allow a bigger hook to grab some meat rather than a little tag of skin. Replacing factory hooks with Owner hooks is money well spent. The points on this brand are sharp from the package and will nicely complement the fish that you have already recorded on your tag.

It's hard, but not impossible, to find a good combination plug rod and casting rod. The plug rod will work best if it has a springy tip that will double the action of the lure with a good harmonic, but it must have enough backbone to set the hook while the rod is still in the holder. A quality line with little or no stretch works very well to communicate the lure's action to the rod and have the rod send it back, unmuted. This is where a good Spectra line of about thirty pounds will count as money well spent. This line should be the main line only, however. I have found it works out better for hooking spooky fish if a monofilament line is used as a bumper between the lure and the braided line. A high-quality swivel placed between these two lines and about six feet of monofilament will assure more takes but still communicate the lure's action back to the rod. The Uni-knot also works well in this setting.

There are several dangers when fishing with plugs. They have a bad habit of flying out of the water when being reeled in either with or without a fish. Close to the boat, keep the rod in a position that will allow the plug to fly away from people if the fish comes unbuttoned. If there is not a fish on when reeling in, just point the rod at the lure when it's close to the boat and the lure won't pop out of the water. To prevent tangles during transportation, use a Velcro wrap around the lures if they are going to stay on the rod or simply remove the lures. Several sets of treble

When I look at this picture I can remember catching steelhead
on each of these plugs under extremely varied conditions.
There is never any doubt about what just happened
when you get a hit on a plug!

hooks bouncing in a boat or pickup can turn into quite a
mess very quickly. Take a few seconds and cover or remove
the lures.

Casting Plugs

Bass fishermen have been doing it for centuries.
Steelheaders have only recently caught on. A typical
bass plug has two treble hooks of dubious quality slung

underneath. These have to go. After removing the factory hooks, install a small split ring at the lure's closest attachment point, then place a small high-quality barrel swivel below that. Last, attach a siwash hook to each of these swivels and you are ready to fish. Most of the lures you would pull behind a boat while back-trolling are suitable to be cast with siwash hooks. No lure will last long around a river filled with wood, but these modified plugs are amazingly resistant to snags on rocks. Having siwash hooks on the swivel means that as the plug is working, the hook point faces away from snags rather than toward them. The current turns the hook so that only the bend of the hook comes in contact with rocks. Spoons and spinners stir up steelhead to a significant degree, but they can't stay in one place very long without getting hung up. The flotation of the plug and any rattle that it may have will bring out the worst in any lurking steelie. The flotation allows the plug to linger in an area just long enough to become insufferable to the fish; that's when the fun begins. The best guides seem to always be tinkering with these lures. They get the heck beaten out of them by the bottom anyway so have a little fun and modify the colors with a good model paint or permanent felt-tip markers.

The usual place for a plug to be used is a long fish-laden run or tailout in a river. Steelhead like to rest in these areas and prefer to remain undisturbed. Often they can be spotted first by using a pair of Polaroid glasses. Spoons, drift gear and spinners often work well in these areas and can be effective in getting strikes. If you really want to irritate a lethargic steelie into smacking something, a plug is often your best ticket.

Plugs have the advantage of being very noisy because of the hooks beating metal on plastic with every wiggle. Throw a noisy set of beads in the body of the plug and it is often more than a sulking steelie can put up with. The hits leave no doubt about the murderous intentions of the fish and they usually come from almost directly downstream. This technique works very well for both summer and winter steelhead and is one that definitely needs to be added to your bag of tricks.

Professional guide Bob Toman watching over client Debbie McQueen on the Deschutes River. We heard Debbie's holler many times that day on the river as the rod was nearly ripped from her hand with savage takes on cast plugs.

The best way to rig for these critters is to have a dedicated rod and reel just for the purpose. A longish spinning rod with good sized eyes and a decent backbone will do nicely. Pair that with a spinning reel loaded with 20-pound-test braided line and you have a winning combination.

Uni-knot a bumper of 12- or 15-pound mono at the end and you'll have the right combination for the job.

Usually plugs should be cast straight out in front of you then drifted on the surface slightly down river. A little tug on the reel will set the plug to work and get it diving. As it goes down stream the current will get it working and you need only control the plug's progress by controlling the swing into the fish's lair. Start with short casts and lengthen them to hit all the water.

Bill Shake and Dave Eng on the Deschutes.

Strikes will be vicious and you must remember that you are using line with no stretch. Too much hookset can result in a broken rod or lost fish. Only a little experience is necessary with this method before you get really good at it. It's a favorite of guides for its simplicity and effectiveness.

When you get hung up, and you will, release about ten feet of line. This causes the line to be pulled downstream from the snag. Give the rod a sharp pull upstream and the lure will usually pop free. If not, the line and leader combination will usually be strong enough to bend the single hook or break the stick free. Seldom do you lose the whole rig.

Jigs and Worms

Bass fishermen gave us something else to successfully fling in the direction of steelhead: jigs, worms and jigs with worms.

Canadians have known for years what we in the lower 48 are finally figuring out—pink worms catch steelies. A four- to six-inch bubblegum pink rubber (plastic) worm either drifted below a bobber or on the back of a jighead will unsettle lockjawed steelhead into making an often fatal mistake. That big ol' bodacious worm scuttling along at or near the bottom is just too good to pass up. Billions of bass have met up with fishermen through a yearning for bubblegum. We can be fairly sure they have not seen one in the wild, but steelies do like pink—a lot! An undulating, twisting, writhing pink playpretty to a bored steelhead might be just the ticket. When you have drifted and plugged a slot that just has to have someone home, try throwing them a curve with a bubblegum worm. Be careful, though, because when you land him you may have to give it the Heimlich to get him to cough up that worm.

Every year I see more people using bobbers with jigs. This is a deadly maneuver that puts the offering at the right depth with a downstream drift that can be extended half a football field. Bobber and jig guys need to have a serious concentration fetish. If you are watching the bobber you don't get to admire the scenery. Too much scenery admiration results in takedowns with no payoff.

Commercial jigs are available specifically designed for presentation to steelhead. They are available in all the right sizes and colors with an excellent selection of hooks. These jigs will rattle a steelhead's cage while saving the fisherman a lot of money by avoiding snags. The bobber gets the bait right where it needs to be and instantly lets the fisherman know of the take. With a good setup and a little practice it can turn a neophyte into an expert in just a few trips.

My favorite style of jig is made with yarn. Yarn holds scent really well and is best used in low water because it has a fairly small profile. I like to use jigs that have a painted head. I sometimes use contrasting colors to attract even more attention. Many of the rules that apply with lures work with jigs. In stained or murky water, darker colors work well because of the silhouette effect. On bright days use bright colors and on dark days use something with color, slightly muted, or just plain black. High water requires a large jig to attract attention and low water means going with a smaller profile.

Rabbit-hair jigs have a really seductive quiver under a bobber. The little wavelets that bounce the bobber have the same effect on the jig. The bounce given by the bobber supplies an unbelievable amount of action to the lure. I prefer a palmered jig to the larger profile of schlappen. Palmered jigs retain a leech-like action that's really seductive, while schlappen provides a large profile and screams color that's easily viewed at a greater distance. Keeping these various attributes in mind when selecting a jig's color and pattern assures more takedowns. If you add scent to a jig, end the day with a little Lemon Joy or Dawn dishwashing liquid to clean the scent off before it becomes rancid and mats down the feathers, fur or yarn.

If fishing in an area that has few snags you can get all the benefits of drift fishing by pulling a jig through a lie without the swing. Opening the bail of the spinning reel or

Jeff Hobson on the Lewis River in Washington landed this chrome buck on a Marabou jig under a float.

A custom hand-tied
marabou jig in peach
and white.

A pink Marabou jig with
beads; an ideal jig for winter
steelhead in1/8- or 1/4-ounce
weights.

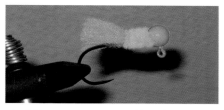

A 1/8-ounce yarn jig tied on a
1/0 Owner jig hook. Yarn jigs
work especially well when
scents are applied as the yarn
will not mat down from the
oil in the scent. This jig in
pink, cerise and white is my
personal favorite.

For low clear water conditions
in winter this 1/32-ounce
jig is ideal.

Rabbit fur works extremely
well for a pulsating jig in low
visibility situations where a
big profile is needed.

Summer-run steelies love
red marabou jigs tied with a
black hackle feather.

An all-around favorite jig for summer and winter fish: marabou with beads tied in 1/8 ounce.

A great low-water pattern: black marabou bead jig tied with blood red beads.

Chenile makes a great body material on this black and red sixteenth ounce jig.

The marabou feathers on this jig were palmered to give the lure a very large profile needed in high or turbid water.

pushing the release button on the level-wind allows the cast to be extended to the limit set by the hook-setting ability of the fisherman. Care, however, must be taken not to impinge on the fishing areas of others in the vicinity.

One of the more interesting ways of fishing a jig is to tie it directly to the end of the line and cast it without a bobber. The best fishermen who use this technique look as if they have a neurological disorder; their rods are continually twitching while the jig is retrieved. The jigs are made of marabou feathers or rabbit hair and the jig head is

A wild Sandy River buck landed on a yarn jig laced with scent.

usually 1/4 ounce. They cast the jig to the far side of a deep pool when the water level is fairly low to very low. When fish are concentrated and won't respond to drifted baits,

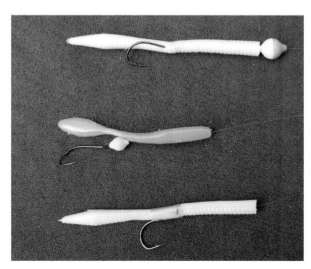

I'm never sure why steelhead hit worms but they do and that is all that matters. For some reason they seem upset when they suck in a pink worm and all of a sudden they want to be in the next river system over.

57

spinners or spoons, they will jump all over those jigs. If a jig is just drifted it immediately becomes snagged. If a jig is cast, allowed to sink and then retrieved with a constant twitching, fish seemed to feel an obligation to bite just to rid themselves of the nuisance. This technique should work in other water conditions but seems to work best in low, clear water where the fish are concentrated. This is an extremely effective technique when conditions are right.

Spoons

When I was much younger and a lot less savvy, I chose to fish for steelhead only with spoons. I had a hollow fiberglass rod that was 8.5 feet long. The rod had very big eyes to accommodate the D.A.M. Quick 220 spinning reel. I still use this combo today and find it works just as well as ever. It's my rod with the longest casting ability.

Many people believe that fishing with spoons is almost as much an art as fly-fishing. This might be stretching it a little but a good spoon-fisherman has many talents that mimic those that fling feathers.

Spoon-fishermen are very concerned about their lines, rods, reels and presentation. The rod must have enough backbone to be able to cast a 3/4-ounce spoon across a broad river into the teeth of a nasty east wind. It needs a long butt section on the handle to cradle under the forearm on those long retrieves and even longer battles with monsters hooked way down river. The rod should have eyes large enough to allow monofilament to slip through easily but not so large that the line will slap on the rod during a hard cast. The tip should be sensitive enough to reveal action of the spoon to the fisherman but stiff enough to resonate to the pulse of the spoon.

The spinning reel for a spoon rod must have a fast retrieve, smooth action and good balance. When the bail is engaged following a cast, the line should return to the position closest to the handle when anti-reverse is activated. This eliminates fumbling for the line when one wants to grasp it with their index finger. This gives an even better feel as the spoon is allowed to traverse the tailout without the reel handle being

Given these spoons I can plan on catching steelies in about any water conditions. Green and blue work best in summer or low clear water in winter. Red-and-white ones work pretty well any time and orange or yellow work well in low light or dirty water.

turned. A "quick-fire" bail system saves additional fumbling and provides for trouble-free, one-handed casts. I prefer a rear drag system on the reel. If fighting a really big fish having the drag in the back expedites changes without having to stick your hand in front of a moving spool.

Monofilament line is my preference when spoon fishing. My favorite over the years has been Maxima Ultragreen; it has really good tensile and knot strength. The color matches the water I like to fish most with spoons—steelhead green. It stands up well to abrasion and is limp enough to cast very well. I have recently begun using Spectra lines on spinning reels for chinook with excellent results. I have tried Spectra lines in lighter tests for steelhead and find they work really well for long casts. Monofilament has a great deal of stretch when fifty yards is off the reel and there's belly in the line. Spectra lines snap a spoon into the side of a jaw on long casts much better than mono but the spoon can't be tied directly onto the end of the line. I have not noticed any inordinate line wear on the guides of my spinning rods when using Spectra lines and it may replace mono as my favorite.

Most effective spoon-fishing is done in water less than ten feet deep with very little color. It's also an excellent technique when rivers are low. Rapids, riffles, slots and boulders are the battleground where spoons excel. Tailouts are the home turf for spoons. Fish lounging in a nice lie are not apt to take kindly to an interloping spoon. Steelies get really testy when the spoon comes into their zone. They don't hit the spoon as hard as a hot shot, but they will remove the rod from your hands if you aren't careful. Most of my spoon takes happen when the lure is at least 45 degrees downriver and being retrieved. Winter steelies like to follow a spoon a good distance but summer fish seem to explode out of nowhere and engulf the spoon with a violent strike.

Luckily this was a hatchery fish because the spoon was completely swallowed and release would have been difficult.

Spoon-friendly steelhead will usually be lying below the boundary layer in a stream. The water above them may be moving quite rapidly but the water in which they are resting will have little flow. For best results the spoon should not be in the fast-moving, upper strata of the river but down where the fish live—in the boundary layer.

Spoons are relatively expensive. One can't afford to go through too many of them in a day without putting a dent in the wallet. If fishing a known stretch of water a good spoon-fisherman will know just exactly how long to let the lure sink before beginning the retrieve. A trick to try in unfamiliar waters changed by recent flooding is removing the hook, or have a spoon always ready without a hook. Make the cast, allow the spoon to sink and count off the seconds until bottom is reached. Replace the hookless spoon with one better armed and decrease the sink time by a second or two. This will save a lot of spoons and give you a better feel for bottom structure and depth. The downside of this is making your first cast into a likely area with a spoon that can't hook a fish. Many is the time I've had a really good "THUMP" on a spoon with no hook. One way to reduce this problem is a spoon painted flat black. Use the stealth spoon for your recon work and put on the pretty stuff to attract a customer.

Once you have an idea how deep the water is and when you need to start your retrieve, you need to determine the boundary layer. The spoon will have a definite throb to it as it swings across the tailout or slot. If you reduce your retrieve speed the spoon's rhythm will slow. If allowed to sink, the spoon will eventually hit bottom. Just before bottom contact, the spoon's pull and rhythm will slow even more. This is when you are within the boundary layer. In deeper water the layer is thick, but in the lip of tailouts it can be very thin. Keeping the spoon in this layer without hanging up is an art form worth perfecting. A fish approached by a spoon at eye level is much more likely to strike than one that looks up at a distant offering well overhead.

"Back reeling" is a technique I've used for years with a great deal of success. If the current is too strong, or if there leep slot in the river, back reeling will allow you to get down through the boundary layer and to those fish lying in the slot. Make your usual cast and retrieve. When the lure is over the area where you want the spoon to dive, turn the reel handle backwards until the spoon touches bottom. Immediately begin reeling forward again. The spoon will have fluttered backward, hit bottom and definitely attracted some attention. It will then take off in a different direction due to the slack line pulling it downstream. If there are eyes watching there is an excellent chance this trick will illicit an immediate attack.

Spoons come in a multitude of sizes and colors. For summer steelhead I use blue and green metallic finishes when the water is clear. They seem to be less intimidating to fish which are easily spooked under these conditions. For winter steelhead or summers being chased under winter conditions, I prefer the red-and-white "daredevil" pattern. This pattern is highly visible and slightly imitates spawning colors. My other favorite pattern is chartreuse with orange spots. This scheme works very well in high or turbid water. Quite often salmon nail this spoon when used for steelies.

In low, clear conditions I often use smaller spoons. These, again, are less intimidating and produce a smaller "thump". Winter fish are treated to smaller offerings if the water is low and clear. When the stream is up or running with some color, I like to use bigger spoons because I need the extra sink and a harder thump to catch their attention.

Spoons are best used with a wobbling action; they should not be allowed to spin. When retrieving the lure at the end of a cast, get it to the surface and slide it across the top of the water. A rotating lure will fill the line with twists making casting very difficult. The lure should always be attached to, the line with a snap and NEVER a snap swivel. The lure's main action begins at the front and is accentuated as it's pulled through the water. The additional drag of a snap swivel retards this action and reduces the wobble of the entire lure. Attaching the spoon to the line directly invites line breaks at the worst possible time. Having a small snap between the line and lure allows the spoon to hit rocks

We drift fished this section then ran plugs through it without success. We had the river to ourselves so I rowed back up to the top. Third time was the charm using a 1/2-ounce green Steelie right on the bottom for this wild hen.

without bruising the line. It also allows for a quick change of hardware.

Line twist is a fact of life whenever a fish pulls the drag on a spinning reel. To get rid of line twist, simply attach a piece of pencil lead to the snap, cast it several times and retrieve with a twitching action. This will remove the twists and facilitate casting when the spoon is reattached.

When spoons get snagged they can often be released using this technique: Open the bail and allow about fifteen feet of line to unspool. This will go downstream and become taut. Close the bail. When the line tightens give the rod a huge jerk. You are jerking the line from a direction that is at least 90 degrees different from the direction when the snag occurred. Try this at least three times before giving up and breaking the spoon off.

CHAPTER IV

Lines and Leaders

More on Line

A huge amount of money has been spent on line development. I am old enough to remember when braided nylon line came onto the market and replaced cotton/linen lines. (Man, that's old.) Simple nylon isn't so simple anymore. Lines can be soft, abrasion resistant, co-polymer, co-filament, high-visibility, low-vis, Dacron, Spectra, etc.

To pick the right line, one must first consider how and where it will be used. If you are going to be fishing in stained or muddy water, line visibility is not much of an issue. Clear water in bright sun requires a line that's not easily seen. If you're fishing near salt water for fish that have been exposed to few or no lines then line diameter and visibility can be greater. Fishing higher in a river system in low, clear water demands smaller, less visible lines.

A good, all-around line is a low-visibility, 12-pound-test main line with a 10-pound-test leader. In all but the clearest waters this will get you into fish and allow you to get back most of your snagged baits. I feel a clear or light-green colored line is about the best and will work in the greatest variety of watersheds. In all situations I believe it's extremely important to use the smallest and least visible leader you can safely use to land fish. The leader material should also be soft, but it must have good knot strength and abrasion resistance. This statement was brought home only two days before I wrote these words. I hooked and landed a 41-inch buck that went about 25 pounds in low and very clear water. The fight lasted nearly a half hour because I was using 8-pound line and leader. Had I used a larger leader I probably wouldn't have hooked the fish. The day before this fish was landed I hooked two fish that would not be budged from the middle of the river. I'd gain some line and they would take it back. On both occasions I lost the fish to abraded leaders cut by their teeth, BUT I hooked the fish. Line and leader diameter and visibility are a tradeoff.

Skinnier leader equals more hookups while bigger leaders can mean more fish landed.

Nylon

For a good all-around line, monofilament nylon is hard to beat. Even the best brands are relatively inexpensive. It's easy to find, has good knot strength, can have low or high visibility, casts well, and is available in limp or hard anti-abrasion varieties. Nylon makes excellent leaders that will hold larger fish in smaller diameters. A good knot will yield a breaking strength 100% of the rated breaking test. If the leader is matched to the water being fished visibility can be kept to a minimum.

For main line, nylon also works well. In the more limp varieties it can be made to cast well and not leave coils of line blowing in the wind. Most nylon lines have at least some memory, and can have a bad habit of coiling off the spool of a spinning reel at the most inopportune time. On level-wind reels all nylon will have some memory in your first few casts. This coiling will usually come out after a little exercise, but can be a problem for the first few casts in the morning. Nylon is prone to dramatic stretching. Trying to break monofilament line loose from a stubborn snag can even pull a drift boat off anchor. It's like a rubber band that can leave you frustrated and with a nasty line cut. This stretch is not altogether a bad thing. If nylon is used as a leader with some of the less stretchy lines mentioned later, it can act as a shock absorber that will save broken leaders and even broken rods. Nylon is like an old pickup truck: it is tested, reliable and doesn't cost an arm and a leg.

Fluorocarbon

I have had a love-hate relationship with this line. I believe its few advantages over nylon do not justify the expense to use it as a main line. For a leader, however, it is unbeatable. The stuff just disappears in most water conditions. It's definitely the stealth approach when dealing with finicky biters. It is quite soft, but not very abrasion resistant. Teeth can make short work of too light a leader material.

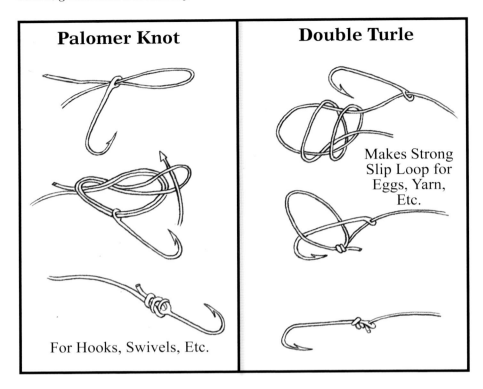

Palomer Knot	Double Turle
	Makes Strong Slip Loop for Eggs, Yarn, Etc.
For Hooks, Swivels, Etc.	

This material will have a diameter that is only about 75% of that of similar test-rated nylon. Using a fluorocarbon leader definitely increases the number of hits you will get in situations requiring unseen leaders; too light a leader will reduce the number of fish you'll land. The downfall of this leader material is the high cost and knot strength. All brands I have tried have poor knot strength compared to nylon. This can be overcome on some brands by tying the appropriate knots: knots that do NOT cause one layer of line to cut into another. The knot I recommend is the Palomar. It's easily tied, and good for both swivels and hooks. It is a bit of a problem, however, if you want to use an egg loop on your hook. To overcome this, you can use a higher line test. Fluorocarbon lines are smaller, so you can move up one or two notches in pound test and still have the same diameter. Fluorocarbon lines are also softer, so moving up in line strength still leaves you ahead of the nylon. Fluorocarbon is nearly invisible, even in a slightly larger size than your usual nylon choice. The answer seems to be to use a bigger diameter leader to gain the advantage of low visibility and retain the softness. Not a bad tradeoff if you need the low visibility.

I have found it a necessity to shock test my leaders made from fluorocarbon. I usually pull on my nylon knots to test them after tying. A remarkable number of them break; it's best to know this before testing it on a bite or snag. With fluorocarbon I not only pull-test the knots, but jerk-test them too. Hold the line and the hook firmly and safely. Give the line a sharp jerk imitating a hook-set, making sure the hook is not pointed toward a finger or your face. A remarkable number of these knots will also break with very light shock even though they stood up well to the pull test. Try it several times, THEN tie it on your line. Better to be glad you did than sorry you didn't.

Spectra Lines

This material is famous for its use in bulletproof vests. Spectra has virtually no stretch and no memory. For the same diameter it is many times stronger than nylon. Visibility is a problem in that it is an opaque material and can only be colored to reduce its ability to be seen. It floats like a fly line and this makes it an excellent choice for use with a bobber. With no stretch it works even better as a line for pulling plugs behind a boat. The natural rhythm of the rod doubles the action of the plug, giving an amazing harmonic to attract or aggravate a resting steelhead. Like all good weapons, however, it must be used properly. Due to its small diameter and abrasive nature it can be hard on inexpensive rod guides. With no stretch it can snap the rod if a bite turns out to be a snag. The line will not break, but the rod will. Spectra lines can cut fingers and hands in an instant if improperly used. Knot strength on Spectra is excellent, but the wrong knots will come untied. The right knot, backed up with a little super glue, will last all season, the wrong knot just comes loose. The reason for knots coming untied is that the line has no stretch or memory, it's very limp. It is the friction of the line tied in a knot that holds it together. The line does hold knots very well when you do not want them to hold. Backlashes and wind knots can be a problem with Spectra lines and can be very difficult to get loose. These lines are very useful in the right setting and can be used on spinning and level-wind reels. If you want a limp, floating line with no stretch and no memory, Spectra lines are the way to go.

It doesn't happen often but on rare occasions you'll get spooled. The knot holding the last two feet of line on the spool of your reel may determine if you'll land what might be the biggest fish of your life or go buy some new line. That knot can be important, so here's how you tie it.

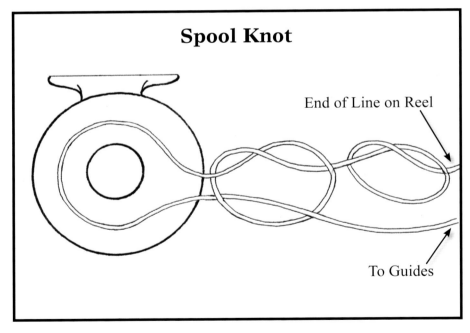

Spool Knot

End of Line on Reel

To Guides

It doesn't happen very often but occasionally you get spooled by a really big fish. The knot holding your line to the reel will make the difference in whether or not you turn that fish around or donate all your line. This is an easy knot for both spinning and level wind reels.

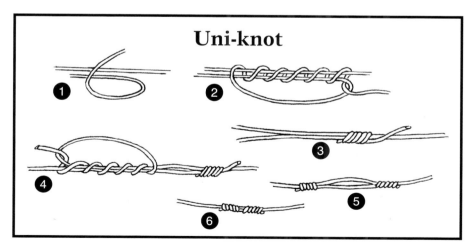

When tying different types or strengths of line
together the uni-knot is one of the strongest.

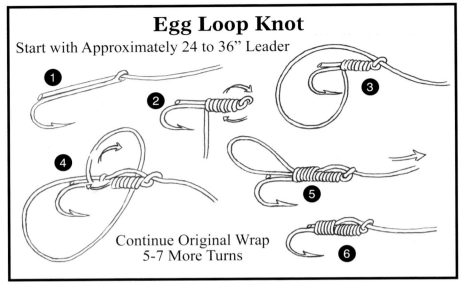

Egg Loop Knot

Start with Approximately 24 to 36" Leader

Continue Original Wrap
5-7 More Turns

*The egg loop knot comes in handy for many things besides
just adding eggs to your hook. It can be used for making
mooching leaders, placing yarn or other bait
below your drifter, or on the hook alone.*

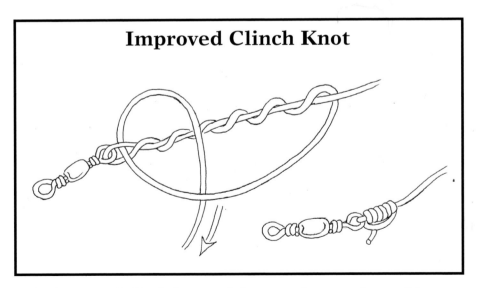

Improved Clinch Knot

*The improved clinch is one of the most frequently used knots.
It is quick to tie and adaptable to many circumstances.
With practice you can learn to tie it in the dark.*

New Line

If you do a lot of fishing you will change your line fairly often. Each line has its own peculiarities and must be put on the spool properly to avoid problems. Spectra lines are small in diameter and are nearly unbreakable. This means that a snag will cause loosely wound line to cut into the spool and go below and into the remaining line. If the line is properly wound initially, the chances of this happening are much smaller. Use the knot shown on page 68 to attach the line to the spool. With light tension begin winding the line on the spool. Overfill the spool and then go outside where there are trees. Attach the line to a tree trunk with a slip knot. Make sure you pick an area that is not frequented by people or dogs. Take a hike. Open the bail or spool on your reel and unwind the line that is on the reel. Go clear to the end and begin retrieving the line. This time, apply the line to the spool under considerable tension. This will dramatically reduce the chances of the line cutting into the line on the spool. When you get back to the line package you may find that the overfilled reel now actually needs more line. Put the needed line on the reel and enjoy the new Spectra instead of fighting with it.

Monofilament line should get the same tensioning treatment as the Spectra but not to the same extent. To wind mono onto a reel you can purchase a device that sticks to a counter with suction cups, holds the line spool and has a tensioning device that will spool the mono on very smoothly. This will evenly tension the line on the spool but it will not strain the line nor will it remove coils built into the line when it was applied.

How many times have you put new line on a spinning reel only to have it flop off the spool while the bail is still closed? It usually takes about ten to fifteen yards of brand-new line and trashes it. To eliminate this problem and to strain your line, do the same trick as above with the new line. Tie one end of the line to a tree, pole, doorknob, anything. Back away about a hundred feet and close the bail on the reel. (Note: Do not allow the line to come off the reel with the bail closed as you'll be adding twist.) With the bail closed, hold on to the spool to keep the line from coming off and walk away slowly to tension the line. You will stretch the mono and at the same time take out some of the twist. Before you come to the breaking point of the line stop walking and give the line several harder pulls. This hardens the line and will eliminate much of the stretch that happens when you need a good hookset. Stand the rod in a safe place and remove your line from the point of attachment at the other end. Go

This line tensioner has suction cups on the bottom that allow it to stick to a counter or other smooth surface. It will allow you to put perfectly seated line on your reel with a minimum of twist.

back to the rod, pick it up and reel in the line. Be careful not to damage the new line on corners or rocks. Using two fingers, tension the line and rewind it on the spool. Your new line will stay on the spool and not come flying off in all directions by itself.

Most homes with telephones have a line-tensioning device within them. Phone books work well because they are heavy and available. Simply tie the new line to the reel. Place the line within the pages of the book toward the spine and start reeling. If there is too much tension place the line closer to the top of the book. If more tension is needed place it deeper. Need even more tension, put another book on top.

Ever notice how the line is twisted on your spinning reel after you've landed a large fish that has taken a lot of drag? Each time the spool goes around a full twist is applied to the line. If the fish is taking that much drag it's either really big or the drag is too loose. Set the drag properly and this won't happen as often.

If you have been fortunate enough to tag a really big one you might want to take a minute to cut your terminal tackle off and straighten your line. This can be done by crimping on a short but straight piece of hollow-core lead. Cast the line several times with the lead only and retrieve very fast. The lead will spin in the water with the fast retrieve and remove the twist. When you lift the lead out of the water leave some line dangling and see if the lead is still spinning. If it is, cast again.

We've all had a loop on the spool of our spinning reels come off with the main line. This usually results in a mess and pulling off more line from the front of the spool is probably going to result in your line being lost if you are not really lucky. This is usually the result of twisted or new line and the remedies described above will often fix the problem. If you look down and see this has just happened and there is not too much line involved there is an easy solution that will usually work. Instead of pulling line off the reel from the front of the spool, pull it off from the side. This will remove only the main running line from the spool and will leave the offending loop still wrapped until you get to the bottom of the loop when it comes off too without a knot. Try it!

Knots

It makes no difference what quality of line you use if you use the wrong knots or poorly tied knots. For steelhead fishing there are a total of six knots one must know. Only three of these are used frequently.

Care must be taken with all knots tied to ensure the knot will hold now and later. It is a sickening feeling to have a knot break or unravel as a huge steelhead cartwheels away trying to throw your hook. Take an additional few seconds to make sure your knots are lubricated and smooth. Test

A flock of hatchery "punch outs" landed while sidedrifting. Guides can go from a broken-off rig to having the client back in the river in less than a minute by tying a simple clinch. It is a fast and effective knot that holds up well under fighting fish. Carefully inspect the sides of these steelies and see how many have been marked by seals.

the knot: Without cutting or hooking yourself, test the knot you've just tied. Better that it breaks for you than to have a fish do it.

Monofilament line is easily bruised while tying knots. If the knot is tied too quickly the line may be burned when it is cinched down. A drop of water will eliminate the heating and act as a lubricant to assure a quality knot. Saliva works well for this purpose but the line has probably been in the water and exposed to things that come out of beavers and cows. Maybe you might want to use a drop of water.

When tying the knot, make sure all the twists and wraps are lying properly and not crossing over each other. This crossing causes a bind that allows one strand of line to cut into another. A pull test and a shock test are advisable once any knot is completed. Pulling will let you know the knot will not break under simple stress. Shock testing tells you the knot will stand up to a snag or a jumper. It is essential that you avoid hooking yourself or others when doing these tests. BE CAREFUL! Failure to test any knot allows the steelhead to test it for you. This might not be the wisest of choices. Take another five seconds and do it right.

If you had to know only one knot it would be the improved clinch. With it you can tie line to hooks and swivels or attach a lure to your main line. This is a knot with excellent strength and a low failure rate if properly tied.

CHAPTER V

Hooks: The Business End of Things

The most basic part of the whole operation and the sharp end of the process is the hook. A lot of thought should go into the selection of hook(s) for whatever type of fishing you are going to do. The following are things to be considered when making your hook selection.

Style

Basically, a hook is a piece of wire with a point and maybe a barb. What is done with that wire is very important to the outcome of your fishing trip. The hook must accommodate the bait or terminal gear and still provide enough clearance to allow the point to penetrate. Once the point is in, the hook must be properly designed to hold the fish during the struggle. The wire must be of sufficient diameter not to bend and the steel must be strong enough to hold a point but not so brittle as to break. Hooks must conform to the regulations prescribed in the area in which you are fishing. They must accommodate the bait and not get snagged in the bottom or in woody debris too often. Hooks must be selected for catch and keep or catch

I wouldn't try to put two dozen leaders into a Pip's but I do believe these are one of the best purchases a steelheader can make. They are one of the many items available that keep your line in the water longer.

and release. Many lures that come with hooks attached have inadequate hooks to properly land steelhead. Some of the most popular steelhead lures originally caught bass and usually these hooks are too small to work well for steelhead.

Size

Size *really* does matter: Talk to six different fishermen or guides and you'll get six different opinions as to the best size hook to use with any particular bait. My opinion is that if you are fishing the lower portions of a river you use larger hooks and larger drift or terminal gear. The fish haven't been exposed to as much gear and they are not as shy as they will be in the upper river after seeing many different offerings. If the water is turbid, larger hooks and terminal tackle can be used. Low, clear water mandates the use of smaller, less visible hooks and baits. Fish will naturally be spookier and a subtle presentation will be most productive. My favorite set-up is a number 2 or number 1, dull-colored, bronze egg hook and a size 12 Corkie. Nearly all of my steelhead will be landed on this combination with only the use of scent and seldom the addition of bait. When I'm plugging I like to replace the original hooks with slightly larger hooks and I usually add an oval split ring or a swivel to distance the hook from the body of the lure. The hook may or may not have a barb depending if the fish will be kept, but it is ALWAYS of a low visibility color.

Color

Painted hooks have been on the market for years and in the appropriate setting they work better than a plain hook. When attraction is necessary a brightly colored hook will give that extra little glint that just might cause a strike. When subtlety is needed, a small, plain bronze hook usually works best. A gooey gob of eggs below a bobber usually requires a brightly colored hook and a size 14 Corkie used in low, clear water will best accommodate a small bronze egg hook. For my own reasons and purely out of habit, I do not use shiny hooks except in salt water for salmon. I either want brightly colored hooks or ones that are not easily seen.

Sharpness

No hook can be too sharp unless it's stuck in your hand. Keep and use a hook file and use it regularly. If you've had a snag or hit a rock, check the hook. It should be sharp enough to catch in your fingernail with only a slight amount of pressure. If it's that sharp it's good to go. If it's not—replace or

Luhr Jensen's Leader Totes are another excellent investment that gives you extra time in the water. Even in cold weather they seem to last forever. This one is probably close to ten years old and has been on hundreds of trips. I prefer the Totes that have Velcro closures rather than the snap.

sharpen it. There are hooks on the market that come out of the box unbelievably sharp. They may be heat treated or chemically treated to sharpen them to a very sticky point. These premium-quality hooks come at a premium price BUT there is no better place to spend your money than on the best hook you can buy. That is the "pointy end" of the spear and the battle starts right there!

Most steelheaders use hooks that are attached to the line with an egg loop knot. These are hard to tie in low light or in wind. There are several devices that will allow hooks to be pre-tied and stored prior to the trip. The Pip's leader dispenser allows up to two dozen leaders to be pre-tied and placed in a tangle-proof container. To use it, simply open the top and pull out a fresh leader. Leader pouches use the same concept of pre-tied leaders but they allow for completely preparing the leader with the drift lure and lead or slinkie. If you are in a situation where it's likely you might lose the whole rig from the lead down, these leader pouches will save a lot of hassle while the bite is on and keep you fishing.

CHAPTER VI
Lead

The ancients used rocks with holes to get the bait to the fish. One of the oldest methods for attaching lead to line involves punching a hole in lead to tie it onto a line. This method is still in use today and is quite effective. Pencil lead is usually 1/4-inch or 3/16-inch in diameter. The lead is either hollow core or solid and is in the form of a wire. Solid-core lead can be cut or broken off to select the right length for the job at hand. A specialized pair of pliers with a small punch cuts the lead and then forms a hole for attaching the line. This is a very simple but effective system. A little more intricate are methods which use surgical rubber to attach the lead to the line. This allows quick changing of the lead without having to tie a knot. Simply pull out one length of lead and insert another more desirable length. Quarter-inch pencil lead is usually used for faster, deeper water where there is less chance of snagging. Due to its larger diameter it will get to the bottom faster and hold better. The larger diameter also allows it to become wedged in wood or rocks more easily. Three-sixteenth-inch lead is used for more subtle presentations in slower water where snags are more likely to happen. It takes nearly twice as much of the smaller-diameter lead to equal the "sink" of the quarter-inch variety.

The big question is how much lead to use. In drift fishing the usual practice is to have the bait just touching the bottom occasionally. The old adage that says "if you ain't losing gear you just ain't fishin" is true. Steelhead are usually found just above the bottom and the lead must be on or near the bottom to be in the strike zone. Fishing most Northwest rivers involves having your lead bouncing over rocks about the size of bowling balls. If they were evenly distributed and the voids were filled with nice sand and there were no sticks or root balls, life would be easier. That ideal drift is seldom found so you better get used to losing rigs.

The usual cast in drift fishing is perpendicular to the bank. The bait is allowed to sink and then drift across the bottom. When the offering is in the "slot" you want to make certain it is near bottom and drifting downstream and not across the current. The more natural the drift the more likely a strike will occur. The lead should be heavy enough to allow the bait to be below the boundary layer and just touching bottom occasionally or not at all. The proper amount of lead is easily determined if you are fishing in a swimming pool. It gets a little more difficult in a river with uneven bottom, slots, boulders, structure and differing water flows both laterally and vertically in the water column. Reading water comes into play here. Experience will tell you about where fish will usually be holding. It is necessary to scale your lead to the drift where you think the fish will lie. Place your cast above and beyond the lie. Allow the current and gravity to get your offering to the lie and let physics do the rest. If you are getting hung up or just dragging the bottom, go with a smaller weight. If you aren't feeling bottom at all, add a little. Casting both upstream AND beyond the drift assures the current will drop your offering into the lie. Casting only upstream of the slot will cause you to only hit the edge of the lie. That belly appears in your line because the faster current in the middle of the drift pulls your bait both downstream and across, unless you are using a bobber. You might think the bait is going down river but it's actually going slightly across stream at the upper end of the cast and completely across the flow at the bottom end of the cast. Most hits occur in the slot or just below it. A significant number of hits will come on the swing at the end of the drift. Give the bait a chance to stop at the end of the drift and rest on the bottom. Quite often a nose has followed the bait all through the swing and is just waiting to pounce at the end of the drift. Let your bait sit for a second or two and then give it the slightest two-inch twitch for dramatic strikes. It's like a cat following a piece of yarn or a feather. If it doesn't move they lose interest. Give it a twitch, however, and they are all over it. Simply reeling in at the end of a cast will take the bait away from fish you never knew were there.

Slinkies

Using slinkies is a method of drift fishing that allows you to fish snaggier water without getting hung up continuously. These simple but effective devices are just parachute shroud filled with lead shot. The diameter and number of shot within the shroud will determine the weight of the slinkie.

Slinkie makers are available that allow easy insertion of the shot into the shroud. These devices make it quick and easy to sit down in front of the TV and put together a six-month supply of slinkies. All that is needed is the slinkie maker, a lighted candle, scissors and a pair of needle-nosed pliers. Fill the nylon with the desired number of shot. Remove the tube from the shroud, heat the nylon until it liquefies and crimp the end lightly with the pliers. Cut off the slinkie from the shroud, melt and crimp the other end. You now have a slinkie. One of the easiest ways of attaching the slinkie to the line is to use a black snap swivel. Open the snap and push it through

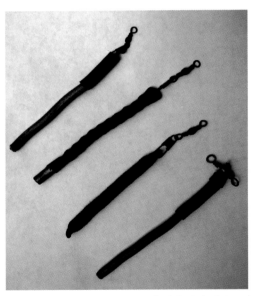

For my lead and slinkie/sinkie hardware I prefer dark or black. We don't want any fish distracted from their mission by bright swivels.

the end of the slinkie. With the snap closed you can either attach the main line directly to the upper loop of the swivel or slide the slinkie onto the line and use it as a slider with a small bead and swivel below to keep it in place above the leader. I prefer black snap swivels because they are less easily seen by fish. Anything that distracts a fish from the intended target at the moment of truth, like a shiny brass snap swivel, is not a good thing to use.

The advantage to using slinkies is they do not snag nearly as often as pencil lead. Their supple nature allows them to slither around and between rocks with little chance of snagging. They are quickly changed without a knot being involved. One of the major advantages to using a slinkie is that they allow the application of scent. The fabric nature of the slinkie body will keep scent working for many casts.

The major disadvantage to using a slinkie is the inability to feel bottom. Lead gives you a constant tic - tic - tic as it goes across the bottom. The slither of a slinkie is harder to feel. What you will feel with a slinkie is the bite, and you'll feel them more often because you are not spending all that time tying on new gear. Many people like to use the slinkie on a sliding rig. If the slinkie to be used is very large this is an advantage because fish would feel the weight on a solid tie and a slider rig is best. If using smaller slinkies, however, I do not feel the extra time to tie up a sliding rig warrants the advantage gained.

Sinkies

These are a little different from a slinkie. The problem with a slinkie is that it's tough to feel the bottom if it is at all smooth. Enter the sinkie. They take a little longer to make than a plain slinkie but they have so much to offer. They

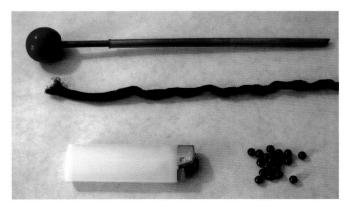

When the rivers are out and the roads frozen, even with the TV on you can sit down and crank out a year's worth of slinkies.

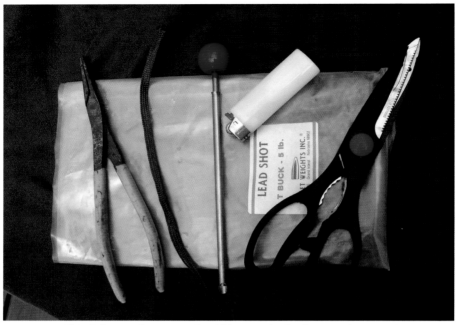

*Slinkie makers make life a whole lot easier and
cost less than ten bucks.*

seldom get snagged up and they allow you to still have the tic
tic feel of the bottom. Here's how it works: Cut the parachute
shroud into lengths about an inch longer than what you want
the finished product to be. If you are making small-diameter
rigs add about three quarters of an inch of 3/16 pencil lead
to the end of the shroud by inserting it half way up into the
nylon. Secure it in place with a little bit of Goop or Shoegoo.
Work the adhesive into the shroud material and have plenty
go down onto the lead that is protruding. Let this dry on wax
paper so it doesn't stick to anything valuable. When it is all
dry add the appropriate number and size shot and complete
the upper end of the weight in the usual way by heating and
crimping. These things are deadly and should be banned.
They give you the advantage of lead and slinkies, plus they
allow you to add scent to the nylon mesh. You spend less
time out of the water, get a better feel for the river and catch
more fish to boot!

Divers

These devices come in many forms. Virtually anything that uses the current to get your bait to the strike zone can be considered a diver. Commercially available divers are offered by several lure companies and they work very well. Using a stout rod with fairly heavy line, simply attach the diver to the end with a knot or a snap. Place a length of leader below the diver and select your favorite bait. The diver is then placed in the stream and back-trolled below the boat. Strikes from divers can be just a gentle nip that looks like a trout or a rod-snapping rip that buries the tip to the water. The advantage of a diver is that it gives the fish a good long look and sniff at the bait. It keeps the bait in the slot without disturbing the fish and it is very simple. Put the diver in the water and allow the rower's skill to keep it in the slot. A disadvantage to the diver is that it allows the fish to swallow the bait. This can be a good thing if you plan to keep the steelie, but a diver and bait should never be used when the fish might be released.

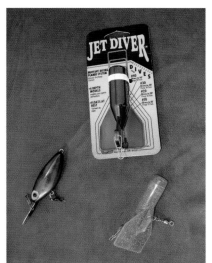

Divers are an alternative to lead that allow your offering to remain near the bottom of the river with far fewer snags.

Larger, diving plugs make excellent divers. The advantage to using a plug is that the action of the plug will be imparted to the bait. Not only is the bait in the strike zone for a protracted period but it has a tantalizing action that drives steelies nuts. If you are going to use any diver you might want to select one with darker colors or even clear. If you are going to use a lure as a diver it would be best if it were painted dark blue or black. Since the diver has no hooks you do not want the steelie becoming distracted by it or, even worse, taking a swipe at it.

CHAPTER VII

Rods, Reels and Techniques

Noodle Rods

Noodle rods can be a hoot. They are best defined as buggy whips or converted fly-rod blanks. The rods are usually ten feet or longer and they are very, very light. Four-pound-test line can be used for really spooky fish, but it is not necessary under normal water conditions. I became a convert around 1995 and noodles are about all I use from shore any more. My favorite rod is my oldest. It cost 39 bucks way back when and has been rebuilt three times. That rod has accounted for literally hundreds of steelhead and I've not found one that can beat it at any price. It's in the two- to eight-pound line class and is 10.5 feet long with medium action. I use this rod for drifting but I do not hesitate to throw on a half-ounce spoon when I see a roll sixty yards away on the other side of the river. The reel is a fast-retrieve spinner loaded with eight-pound test. That lets me cast a mile using a little more weight but I can get away with a slinkie that has just a couple of shot. This rod has landed most of my fish that were twenty pounds or more and has bested a few chinook that showed up at unexpected moments. The extra length acts as a great shock absorber for bigger fish and the medium action has enough backbone to yard in the big boys but still remain delicate for strike detection and lightweight offerings.

My second favorite rod is 12.5 feet long and is definitely not for a beginner. It has a super fast action and is extremely delicate. It does not have enough backbone to cast much weight and is definitely not the rod for anything over 15 pounds of fish. It would not last five minutes in a boat with another angler without becoming a three piece but it is a joy to handle. I can cast super light offerings to the places I need to reach and the fight from an eight-pound steelie is something to behold. When I use this rod I see why fly-fishermen enjoy catching steelhead and tarpon on long rods.

This rod comes out on special days when the spirit needs a little attention. While the rod previously described is used to being dragged through the mud, the blood and the beer, the long rod is for bank angling on special occasions only. One is a GMC and the other a Porsche.

My personal history with steelhead started with a spinning rod. I was trout fishing on the Nisqually River in Washington and I was using a periwinkle for bait. Something grabbed the bait, cleaned the reel, tied me around a branch and left me with knocking knees. The introduction did not last long but the addiction is permanent. A good friend let me try his level-wind one day on the Sandy River. I hooked a steelie in just a couple casts but the drag seemed so foreign until he showed me how to use the "magic thumb" to augment the drag. Thumbing a lightly set drag eliminates a lot of fish lost to line breakage. The thumb has to be educated, however, and the only way to do that is practice fighting fish. The introduction to level-winds was expensive and it still costs me plenty when something new appears. In 1994 I tried using one of the new noodle rods. My fancy was again tweaked and I bought one immediately. The rod was about thirty dollars and the reel cost about the same. I was amazed at how many more fish I was hooking on the noodle rod. It seems when you set the hook with almost eleven feet of rod you are able to move a lot of line in a big hurry. The smaller, lighter line on a noodle rod makes for more strikes and I was able to land large fish on them because of the rod's forgiving, limber nature. I have tested the rod on large steelhead. Thirteen of the fifteen over-twenty-pound steelies I've landed came to the bank on a noodle rod with eight-pound-test line and leader. When I go drift fishing from the bank I now take two noodle rods and a light level-wind set-up. This combination will allow me to have several baits immediately ready and allow the use of new muscles when I switch from one rod type to another.

Whether you are just beginning or are a seasoned veteran of many frothy battles, you should consider getting a noodle rod. They don't cost much and are a very effective weapon. The good thing about noodle rods is that they land lots of fish, even big ones. The bad thing is that they can be very hard on the tendons of your elbows and shoulders. Ten or eleven feet of leverage give steelhead a lot of mechanical advantage. When starting out, you might want to change from one rod system to another throughout the day. This will ease you in to noodling and prevent a chronic and painful condition from developing.

A drift rod with a level-wind reel is pretty much the standard steelhead set up. With a little practice and proper tuning of the reel one can accurately cast these machines and put lures and baits in harm's way regularly. Drift rods come on sale yearly and can be had for under forty dollars. If you become addicted or win the lottery, you might wish to spend a lot more. I appreciate a good-quality cork handle. That material is fairly warm for those frosty mornings and it gives a good grip when the hands are wet. A trigger built into the handle is a necessity. This little device has saved many rods from a watery burial. Chilled hands in fingerless gloves benefit from a rod with a trigger when an enraged chromer tries to rip the rod from your hands. A sensitive tip is a very good thing in a drift rod. For most folks it is the telegraph that turns on the red light in your brain when a steelhead has just taken your bait. To properly set the hook, however, that sensitive tip must expand into a blank that has enough backbone to get the job done. Ceramic guides and tight, well-finished wrappings complete the weapon of choice for most folks when selecting a drift rod.

Low-Rodding

For spinning, noodle and drift rods there is a technique, when properly used, that will easily double the number of fish that you will land. Most people cast across stream, let it sink and then hold the rod at about a 30- to 40-degree angle. This is why that sensitive tip is necessary in a good rod. With the low-rodding technique you could use an eight-foot closet pole and easily outfish someone with the best of rods. This method allows the fisherman to sense when the fish picks up the offering. At this time the fish has the bait in its mouth and the mouth is closed. When most folks feel the bite it's when the fish is violently shaking its head in attempt to dislodge the offending hook and its mouth is wide open. That jerk, jerk, jerk is the fish doing its very best to get rid of your hook. If you are able to set the hook while the fish is tasting and testing the bauble in its closed mouth you have a much better chance of success.

Here's the trick: Don't hold that rod up in the air. Cast, let the bait sink, mend the line, reel up any slack and then point your rod where the line goes into the water. This will work with either level-wind or spinning reels. Place your ring, middle and index fingers on top of the line where it comes off the reel and have your thumb below the line. Do not clasp the line with your fingers and thumb but gently put a bend in the line causing a tension across the fingers and thumb. You will be able to feel every pebble the lead encounters as it touches along the bottom. You will feel the larger boulders and you will feel the leader wrapping around sticks and then releasing. Most importantly, you will feel the difference in pressure on the line when the steelhead removes the drag of the bait from the computation and only the lead drag is left. That is when you set the hook. The fish's mouth is closed and the hook is in place, usually in gristle or bone. Even with bait you will not deeply hook fish because they have not had a chance to swallow.

As the bait and lead proceed across the bottom the bait is downstream from the lead roughly the length of your leader. When the fish takes in the offering with the rod high method you must wait until the lead has gone past the fish. The line will not come tight until the lead has moved about four or five feet. This is plenty of time for the fish to taste and reject the bait and you will never know you had a take. With the low-rod method you feel the original take and set the hook before the fish has any idea it has made a terrible mistake. You will be amazed at the number of hits you never knew you had. You'll also be happy with the number of dinners that come home with you if you choose to invite them.

My first new reel was given to me by my dad in 1963. It was a Mitchell 300 and it has been on hundreds of trips. Every so often I'll pick it up and feel its heavy frame in my

The low-rodding technique works very well to assist the fisherman in feeling even the lightest of bites, but this rod is held too high for best results. The rod needs to be pointed right where the line goes into the water.

In this picture the rod is held a little too low. Holding the rod too low is a technique that works well when there is a cross wind, as less line is exposed to moving air.

Just Right! Notice the fingers and thumb aren't grasping the line but the line just floats on the fingertips. Anything placing any tension on the line will be instantly felt by the fisherman.

hand. I'll turn the handle and sense its slow, unbalanced mechanical workings that were state-of-the-art at that time. For less than that old Mitchell cost forty years ago you can buy a graphite-bodied, balance-handled, high-speed retrieve, ultra-smooth-drag wonder made in China or Japan. Three pages later in the same catalogue you'll see reels that cost twenty times what that Mitchell did. You know what? Properly used they'll all catch fish. The fish don't know what type of reel is working them toward the bank. They just know they have to resist it or die in the trying. You don't necessarily get a lot more reel for your buck when you are buying a spinning reel. What you probably will get is a reel that lasts a lot longer for that extra money but you could use the same amount of money to buy several reels and still be ahead with the less expensive model.

I have found that the extra bucks *are* well spent when buying a bait-casting reel. More bearings, smoother drag and longer, tangle-free casts are the product of a better-quality reel that has to cost more initially. Level-wind reels

A nice pair landed using just a corkie, scent and the low-rodding technique. If you perfect this drift technique you will be amazed at the number of strikes you never knew you were getting. The other advantage is that you are moving a lot more line on the hookset and stand a better chance of a hookup on each jerk.

are extremely intricate. Failure to lubricate regularly or the addition of one grain of sand can wreck your whole day if you have only one reel with you. The drags need yearly maintenance and the reel must be properly tuned and adjusted to assure trouble-free casts. Why go to all this trouble? Because the reel feels sweet in your hands. That perfect cast mastered by hours of practice, placed into the perfect drift and attacked by a steelie that demands its freedom. The spool whirling under your thumb, the intricate ballet of pump and reel...pump and reel all come together with that silver-sided beauty beached at your feet. Talk to any fly-fisherman who has landed a steelhead; their eyes get glassy and they stare into the distance as they describe the experience. The same process applies as you try out a new method of catching steelhead on equipment foreign to you. A whole new chapter in your sport begins.

Spinning reels enable you to cast greater distances with less weight. They will often outcast the best level-wind under conditions requiring smaller weights or smaller lures like jigs, spinners and spoons. Nearly as important as the reel is the type and weight of line used. Heavier lines impede accurate, long-distance casts regardless of the type of reel. Lighter and limper lines facilitate these delicate casts but do not stand up as well under the stress of snags and abrasive bottoms. Heavy water demands bigger, heavier lures and weights. The higher-pound-test lines come into their own under these conditions. Bait-casting reels work best with moderate to heavy weights.

Extendodrift

One of my favorite tricks to keep an offering in the slot longer is the "extendodrift". Once the cast has been made to the far side of the drift I let it settle to the bottom. When the line comes about even with me I trigger the reel and allow line to come off the spool. This forms a belly in the line but also allows the terminal tackle to drift downstream and not swing across the current. This keeps the business end in the slot for a much longer drift. It also puts a much larger belly in the line. With a mend or two I can remove some but not all of the bellied line. This is where the low-rod method really pays off. Even a solid take will feel mushy and any hookset has to be of the mightiest variety. This technique accounts for a lot of fish and should be used frequently. It also accounts for a lot of snags because a lot of line is drifting across the bottom. It is best used where snags are at a minimum. The extendodrift is best used with a level-wind reel but it can be used with a very smooth and free-rolling spinning reel allowed to turn backwards. With either reel the technique is deadly and it will keep your offering in the "kill zone" much longer.

If I'm in a situation where there is a very long drift well out into the river and my bank is free of obstacles I like to do the "sidewalking" drift. If you can't do two things at once very well this may not be the technique for you. Cast above and beyond the drift. Let the line come downstream until it is even with your body. Tighten the line and walk downstream at the rate the line is proceeding. Keep the rod low and pointed to where the line enters the water while keeping the rod as still as possible. The strikes on these drifts are very subtle. They are usually just a tightening of the line. If this is felt, roar back, set the hook and **reel**! This is one of the few drifts I make that the fish feels me before I feel it. On both the walking drift and the extendo-drift many fish will be hooked on the wrong side of the mouth. This means that the fish were following the hook downstream and took the lure going the same direction. It is good that you get so many hits with these drifts but being hooked on the wrong side makes the hooks prone to pulling out during the fight. Better to have loved and lost, etc...

Try these two techniques. They present the most natural drift you can get without a boat or bobber being involved. If fish are present, these methods are killers and will produce.

When you have a nice long drift and a trail alongside it, try "sidewalking". Cast your drifter to the slot, tighten the line and hold the rod in the hand closest to the river. Point the rod where the line goes into the water while keeping your index finger on the line.

Extended Drift

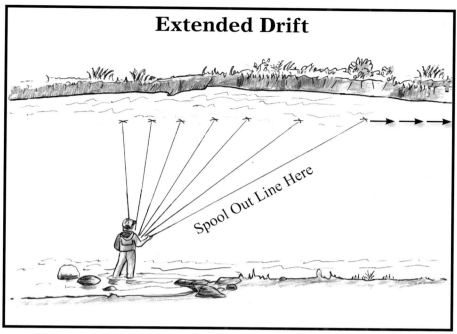

Spool Out Line Here

Sometimes you just can't cast to where you need the presentation to wind up. By allowing your spinning or level-wind reel to spool out line in a controlled manner you can work your offering into downstream areas that are far beyond casting range but easily reached with a drift extention. Note: If using a spinning reel while leaving the bail closed, the reel should have a really loose and smooth action for this to work well.

This is the closest you can get to a natural drift without a boat or bobber. The strikes are usually just a slow tug on the line and the fish feels you before you feel it so you have to be fast on the trigger.

*A nice little buck trying to make good his escape
after falling for the sidewalking technique.*

Sidedrifting

Boondogging, boondoggling or sidedrifting is a similar technique to the two just described. It is different in that there is a boat involved. The boat runs upriver and slows to become stationary in the water but going downstream relative to the river bottom. Baited enticements are cast toward the drift and slightly upstream. The boat is kept in the current and stays roughly even with the bait. Usually this technique is used in faster-flowing, deeper water and it is a killer method that exposes a lot of fish to the bait. The strikes are sudden and hard because the fish was moving downstream and the bait is taken as the fish turns. The fish has stopped and the boat is moving. Hooksets do not need to be hard because the fish will do most of the work themselves. Just lift and reel. Bigger rivers lend themselves to this technique because a lot of high-speed boating is necessary. Concentrations of fish attract concentrations of fishermen. The trip will not usually be an outdoor wilderness experience but may be akin to a fishing trip next to a freeway. You and your guide will want to stay on top of the fish and the rest of the fishermen will feel the same way. **But**, it can be very productive.

On smaller rivers where you or the guide can either motor or row upriver this technique can be particularly deadly. The presentation to the steelhead is primarily a sight offering. The drift rig comes into their field of vision and is gone almost immediately. The fish has but an instant to react, turn, pursue, grab and turn upstream into the current. The strikes are seldom jolting but usually just a strong pull on the line followed by a hookup. Novice and experienced anglers find this method very appealing and guides love it because it is so effective.

If there are just one or two people in the boat it is not really necessary to use a high-visibility main line. If the boat is more crowded then a high-vis line is mandatory. The lines need to be kept apart when drifting to avoid catastrophies that ensnarl several fishermen in an instant. The fish are notoriously uncooperative in keeping the lines separated when they attack, so line visibility is critical.

Using high-vis line means longer leaders are mandatory as well. Spooking fish is easy if the leaders are too short. The best sidedrifters often use four-foot leaders of the most invisible and limp material available. On the business end of the line will be a single- or double-hook rig with very small hooks and a bright floating drifter with maybe just a hint of several eggs or a shot of scent. Remember, this is a sight thing for the steelie but small and subtle is important in most cases unless the water is stained or turbid. Only a very small amount of lead or a short slinkie is necessary. The boat is keeping pace with the current so a very small amount of weight keeps the drifter right where it needs to be. Because the terminal tackle is covering so much territory and steelhead streams are littered with snags, boulders and branches, plenty of weights and drifters must be at the ready to keep the whole process functioning smoothly.

One of the guides I have used many times on the Cowlitz River in Washington could keep the boat ideally positioned in heavy traffic, handle his own rod, hand that rod off to a client when a breakoff occurred, tie up a new drifter and sinker and have the new rig fishing again in less than a minute with a new gob of eggs attached. It was poetry in motion just to watch him perform and we always came back with a limit of fish from a well-managed put-and-take river planted with hatchery fish. Pre-tied leaders, prepared eggs and lots of precut lead or slinkies at the ready will make the trip a pleasure for fishermen and a calamity for fish.

This technique has become a standard on many rivers and is increasing in popularity. The technique is extremely effective but requires covering a lot of water in a big hurry and can result in passing up fish. Fish usually see the bait or drifter for only an instant and this results in strikes that are interesting, to say the least! You may pass by a lot of fish but if the boat is properly controlled and the casters are on their game a lot of fish will see your bait.

In most instances the boat is in the current and casting is done toward shore. In general the largest number of fish in the river will be laying on the seam between faster middle water and slower water at the edge. That is a great place for bait to be placed and every effort should be expended to keep it there while the drift is being made. This game can be played from rafts, drift boats powered by oars and/ or outboards and by jet boats. Purists like to put the boat in the river and silently ply the waters to the take-out. This is an excellent technique, whether using a fly or drift gear, and it makes for a quiet and peaceful day only interrupted by the necessity of reeling in those pesky fish. Throw an outboard on the back of the boat like they do on Chetco and Smith rivers and you get to enjoy the drift again and again, but it is a slow grind back up through the fast water. Add another twenty thousand dollars and we can hit the whole stretch, time after time, in a jet boat. No matter how it's done, sidedrifting is a great way to keep your gear in a fish's face.

The favorite set-up for side drifting seems to be a longish, limber spinning rod equipped with a high-visibility line that allows the boat handler to see where everyone's line is in the water. Most baits are small, as are the weights that keep the gear at a pace that matches that of the boat. Too much weight and the fisherman is continually snagged up. Too little and the rig is off the bottom and quickly working its way back to the side of the boat. A very small piece of hollow pencil lead or a very small slinkie seems to be the favorite for keeping bait in the zone.

Long leaders work very well in side drifting. Smaller diameters work best to keep leader material invisible. Smaller hooks fool fish better and keep the number of snags to a minimum. If you are adverse to losing gear, however, you might want to try another technique. Side drifters often go through twenty or more leaders in a morning's work. These must be tied-up ahead of time and immediately available for instant installation following one of many snags that will occur continually. The drifter should be installed on the leader and hooks pre-sharpened to minimize downtime. If you are fishing a popular side-drifting river you might just see an occasional "Christmas Tree" of lost gear under water. As snagged leaders accumulate they tend to hang up even more customers drifting by and the downward spiral just gets worse with each contribution. Foam leader spools are available that allow fishermen to grab a leader by the end and tie it on in a matter of seconds.

Preferred bait for side drifting is cured salmon or steelhead eggs. Nearly all guides I have side drifted with seem to like a bright pink selection of eggs. They are carefully cut to about the diameter of a dime and are firm enough to stand up to repeated casts and high-velocity contact with the bottom. A small floating drifter assists in keeping the bait off the bottom and in making it more visible to fish.

You have to keep in mind that this is going to be primarily a sight game for the fish. They don't get to take in a big whiff of the bait and ponder very long before they make a dash for it. The takes while side drifting are very satisfying for beginners because there is no doubt about what has just happened, and the fish usually do a good job of hooking themselves.

One method that seems to work well on rivers that do not have a lot of wood or really big rocks is a "Bouncing Betty". This is a hard rubber ball that is dense enough to roll across the bottom but not so heavy that it falls into every crack and crevice. They allow side drifting to be accomplished with a minimum of hang-ups involving the weight and can be a big advantage in keeping an intact bait in the water. If you see these rigs being used you will see nearly everyone using them, or you won't see them at all. Local knowledge comes into play here and you might want to "Do as the Romans do".

Another technique I've seen work with deadly effectiveness is the use of a bobber and bait or a bobber and jig. The nice thing about this set-up is that snags are nearly non-existent. The bobber can either be kept abreast of the boat or allowed to go a little downstream. If the bobber is directly downstream and a snag is encountered a rod can be easily broken by the boat, oars or motor. It is best to keep the bobber out of the plane of the boat until you become really good at side drifting. Steelhead do not usually have a significant amount of time to inspect an offering that is being side drifted. That means the lure needs to be visually appealing for the chase to begin. An "eggy" appearance will be all that much more enticing as it's being homed in on. A wonderful applied smell and/or taste will seal the deal for a take-down and game on!

EZ Eggs are a new product on the market. The manufacturer provides them in fish-attracting colors and they come with a very light shrimp scent. The really attractive part to fishermen and fish, however, is that they are buoyant. The bane of all side drifters are the continuous snags that occur and the time spent replacing the rig and getting back in the game. EZ Eggs have just enough flotation to keep the lure at eye level for fish and just out of reach of snags. They look fantastic when placed as singles on a hook with some complementary yarn, and they can be tied into a knot to simulate an egg gob if a larger visual target is needed. The eggs come in strings of a dozen and their

One of the few times I like to use eggs is sidedrifting. The bait comes at the fish in a hurry and it is a sight thing with a quick grab and a fast stop. With just a drifter the fish has nothing to encourage it to hang on. The juicy eggs stay in the mouth just a second or two longer to assure one to take home.

durability is phenomenal. They are translucent to exactly mimic a natural egg and they are soft and supple to assure some serious munching while the bite is taking place. When they are added to a bit of yarn, or even supplemented with a smidge of natural egg, they are very hard for fish to turn down. Because they come in a string they can be cut into individual eggs for the hook, cut into doubles and placed in the egg loop or tied in a knot for a really gaudy appearance.

My first time out with this bait was on the Sandy River. That day the boat hooked nine steelies with three in the teens and lost only two leaders all day. The second trip with EZ Eggs was on Oregon's coastal Wilson River. Again, only several leaders were lost all day and the boat was limited out by early afternoon. One of the fish made the local sports page, a twenty-plus-pound hatchery fish whose dying wish was for yarn and EZ Eggs. You might want to give them a try as the combinations are endless and the results can put you in the hero column.

CHAPTER VIII
Eggs and Other Baits

Egg Cures

It is not considered good manners to ask another steelheader for the formula to his favorite egg cure. It IS considered appropriate to bribe his wife for the formula or steal it by any other means, but don't ask for it. Some things just aren't done!

Why do steelhead relish the eggs of their own kind? It might be that they ate eggs when they were young and the look and smell of eggs lingers when they are adults. It might also be that as adults they do not want the offspring of others competing with their own progeny so they eat eggs that are not their own. Either way they relish eggs.

Fresh eggs from a mature hen will usually not excite steelhead as much as colored and cured eggs will. Add some red or pink color to eggs that have been cured and slightly dried and you have a deadly combination. Put a drifter ahead of the gob of eggs and you have an even better combination. A smidgeon of yarn to cause the concoction to tangle in their teeth and you've created nearly the ultimate weapon.

Commercially prepared eggs of excellent quality are difficult to come by. Great care must be taken with eggs from the point of harvest to the time they are used. For this reason I prefer to prepare my own eggs and safeguard them until they are used.

When a hen that will be kept is landed it must be properly bled immediately. This is done by breaking a gill with the index finger or a knife after the fish has been knocked unconscious. The heart will continue to beat for about a minute and if the fish is held up by the tail after breaking the gill it will be completely bled out in seconds. When the eggs are removed from the hen they must be thoroughly cleaned of any blood that remains. Failure to do this will result in inferior color when the eggs are cured.

Commercial cures are available that provide excellent results if the directions are followed precisely. I like to use

There are many excellent cures on the market. Find one you and the fish like and experiment with it before moving on to another cure.

cures that allow for freezing the eggs. When eggs are frozen, small ice crystals form inside the egg's outer shell. These crystals pierce the skin and allow for better penetration of the dye. This means the egg will retain its color in the water longer and fewer eggs need to be used. Packing unfrozen eggs into plastic bags and squeezing out all the air without breaking the eggs is a good way to start.

Freeze the eggs in the bags. When they are frozen hard they can be moved to vacuum freezer bags without crushing the eggs. Once secured in the vacuum bags they will last for years in the freezer without any sign of dehydration or burning. Freezing them in smaller quantities will result in fewer eggs being wasted and they'll thaw immediately for use when placed in the stream or left out in the air for a few minutes. Once the eggs are thawed they can be refrigerated for protracted periods if they are kept from open air, which allows mold to form.

For steelhead, smaller is usually better. A big gob of eggs will definitely excite a chinook but steelhead are better tempted with a small offering about the size of a cherry.

For winter fish, eggs must be replaced often to retain their color and scent. For summer fish, quite often only a small skein with maybe an egg or two behind a corkie works very well.

Whether drifting eggs, using them under a bobber, backbouncing or behind a diver it is best to let the fish take them for just a second or two before setting the hook. This allows the fish to get them back into the mouth and virtually assures a good hookset. Striking too early results in a lot of misses, waiting just a second or two assures a much higher success ratio. If you are fishing over native fish that will be released it's best not to use bait at all. If eggs are necessary you do not want to wait too long and allow the fish to swallow the eggs. This will result in serious and maybe even fatal injury to the fish. Hooks in the gullet or deeper can penetrate vital organs outside the digestive system. Besides being painful it will result in a lingering death for the fish.

Sand shrimp are one of the best baits available for steelhead. They often eat shrimp like candy so care must be taken to keep them from swallowing if the fish is to be released. If the fish will be kept and you are not fishing over natives—let 'em eat it!

Sand shrimp behind a diver or under a bobber are hard to beat in most water conditions. They have a great scent and steelies pick them up off the bottom or take them on the drift. It's a bait that can be used under a lot of diverse conditions. The old saying, "better to have and not need than need and not have" applies to sand shrimp. When they won't take anything else they will usually take shrimp. Below are several methods of hooking up shrimp. Their bodies are best described as crunchy Jell-O so they can be hard to keep on the hook. With a little practice you can make a shrimp last through repeated casts or drifts and these examples will help you do just that.

Shrimp are hard to keep alive for more than several hours outside a chilled environment. Heat will kill them in minutes. If the shrimp are to be kept for a full day on the river they must be in a cool, dark place with no freshwater exposure. They are harvested in coastal estuaries with brackish water where they are pumped or dug from their holes on mud flats. When they are placed in confined quarters, like a bait container, they urinate continuously. The ones on the bottom really get a bad deal. That is why the bait containers have a little foam diaper at the bottom. This keeps the ones at the bottom fresher, longer. If you buy shrimp and want to keep them fresh for several days without water use a broad, flat plastic tray with a lid. Place several layers of paper towels in the bottom of the container and lay the shrimp in only one layer deep. Kept refrigerated (cool but not cold) they will last for several days. It is important that they be covered. In the dark they go looking for a hole to hide in.

For steelhead I prefer very small female shrimp. Their color is brighter than the white of the larger male. The smaller females tend to stay on the hook longer and they don't have the large claw to get in the way. When I must use the big males I use only the tails or break off the big claw on the smaller ones to keep it from preventing a hook penetration.

Since sand shrimp are so perishable they are usually used within a day or two of being pumped. There is, however, a method for cooking and brining these critters that makes them usable for months after being processed. They must be boiled in a brine solution for 90 seconds and then allowed

Steelhead Candy!

to cool. They are then frozen in a sealed container and will be usable for months to come. They remain supple after thawing and any color dye can be used to give them the desired hue found most acceptable by your local steelhead. They work well either whole or just using the tail for drifting or under a bobber and they are excellent behind a diver for backtrolling down a river.

Prepared Baits

Powerbait, usually used for trout, now comes in pre-molded, corkie sized baits that will stay on the hook for many casts. These baits would be best used in slower moving water or in deeper pools where fish can get a really good sniff of the aroma. The baits are available in many different colors. They do not have a shelf life but a half life. When you don't have good eggs or shrimp with you and you are fishing slower water you might want to give these little jewels a try.

If good bait is hard to come by and you are fishing faster water you might want to try this technique. Any of your

It is an entirely different story if the fish is going to be kept. Another very good reason to have a black net is that it is not highly visible to other anglers. If you are on one of our crowded coastal rivers you are sure to attract attention (and a crowd) by waving about a bright green net, letting the fish splash repeatedly right next to the boat, noisily landing the fish and then giving high-fives all around while loudly recounting the battle at the top of your lungs.

It is much better to keep the net out of play until the very end. Fight the fish to the boat and make sure it is whipped before slipping the net under the HEAD then quietly bring it into the boat. Netting the fish by the head is using their great forward gear to your advantage. Quickly and quietly subdue the fish and get it in the box. Remember to bleed the fish by cutting or breaking a gill and remember to clean the net and deck where the fish was laying. Steelhead and salmon slime on the deck is one of the best lubricants available for removing standing fishermen from that position.

Boots, Clothing and Keeping Warm

In my younger days I did not mind being cold and I did not mind being wet, but I did mind being cold and wet. I used to disdain the use of waders and would just jump into the stream with a pair of jeans and tennies. After a while I couldn't feel the pain in my legs and could fish in numb comfort. With age comes some wisdom. I now desire in no way to be either cold or wet.

A good pair of insulated hip boots or chest waders is an excellent investment. The waders can double as rain gear and will keep you both warm and dry when butt-deep in a river or riding in a drift boat. Waders come in many different styles and are made from several different materials. For summer fishing a nice set of breathable waders fill the bill. They can be used with a pair of sweat pants and wool socks in waters that are a little cooler. For the frosty-morning winter steelheader there is nothing like a pair of 5mm neoprenes with sweat pants and a pair of cotton socks under wool. Chesties come in two main styles: with or without boots attached. The stocking-foot model gives one the advantage of selecting different shoes or boots. Ankle highs are for light cobble wading or eight-inchers can be used for really good ankle support. The models with integral boots give very little support but they do not constrict the blood flow as much as the stocking-foot types and they go on much more quickly and easily.

What's on the sole of the boot is very important. If you are wading fast-running water with a slippery bottom there is little that will beat cleats. The best way to describe them is 'like a golf shoe.' Cleats give excellent traction but they are really hard on the vinyl deck of most boats and don't work at all in a raft. Felt soles (really nylon) are like a Scotch Brite pad glued to the bottom of the boot. They work well on bottoms that have a lot of algae and slime. They will give you a good hold and keep you standing upright in moderately fast water and on smaller rocks. Lug soles are for walking in mud or where you have to climb around in and out of the water. They will give you traction in mucky stuff but offer little help in fast water or slippery bottoms. Choose your sole wisely or know how to swim well. Make sure you always wear a belt at the top of chest waders. If you do fill your waders it is very difficult to move with an extra hundred pounds of water in the waders with you.

In summer a pair of sunglasses and a little mosquito repellant provide the protection needed. Winter steel-heading in the Northwest demands a little more between you and the elements. Rubberized nylon rain gear had been the standard for many years to keep warm and dry. As long as there was little exercise involved this worked well. Walking into and out of a gorge or rowing a boat can cause enough perspiration that you might as well not be wearing rain gear because you'll be just as wet as without it. New, breathable rain gear makes all the difference in staying comfortable. It breaks the bite of the wind, keeps rain out and wicks perspiration from the body. Warm **and** dry, now, that's a good thing.

We now have you with a warm, dry body and feet but what about those hands? It's pretty hard to keep fishing when your hands feel like they have been run over by a truck, or don't feel at all. An inexpensive item that can make a day's fishing is a pair of fingerless wool gloves. They keep out wind, add warmth even when wet and give you a lot of protection for very little money. Neoprene gloves are relatively inexpensive, allow no wind to get through and are warmer when wet than wool. The neoprene gloves, however, will cut off your circulation unless they fit just right so choose them carefully.

Wool or fleece fingerless gloves provide an amazing amount of warmth and protection from the wind even when wet.

A good, wool stocking cap under the hood of your rain gear will keep the wind from freezing the tips of your ears and prevent an earache. There are caps available that have a bill attached, keeping the rain out of your face in a moving boat and on shore if there is a breeze blowing. This bill can be especially important if glasses are worn.

The chemical handwarmer has been available since the Korean War. Some burn lighter fluid and some have a solid chemical stick that burns for hours. More recently on the market are powdered chemical warmers that slowly combust without fumes or flame. These work only one time and are fairly expensive. The heat produced is low and they are much less likely to cause burning of the skin. If you want lots of heat and don't mind the fumes the combustion handwarmers will do the job. For gentle heat the powdered iron models are the way to go. There are no fumes and you just open the package to get them going. Many of your better coats now have built-in handwarmer pockets that

*One or two of these in your breast pocket will keep your
body warm and provide instantly warmed hands.*

keep your body warm and allow access for your hands when
they are ready for a warming.

They have been on the market for years but due to recent
strides in battery technology they have become much more
effective at keeping hands and feet warm for the whole
day. Electrically powered gloves and foot warmers are
relatively inexpensive and provide a day's comfort in a cold
aluminum boat. I still wouldn't expose them to a lot of wear
with extensive walking and I wouldn't expose them to water
any more than necessary but these devices have definitely
improved. For only a moderate cost they can add a lot of
comfort to an otherwise long, cold day.

An item that will save a slip, trip and a dip is a wading
staff. These are commercially available and can cost up to
a hundred bucks. To secure a perfectly serviceable wading

staff go to Goodwill or Salvation Army. They will have a good supply of ski poles, usually aluminum and in many different lengths. They will have a wrist strap and come equipped with the ring near the pointy end of the shaft. Simply remove the ring and you have a very nice wading staff for practically no money.

Glasses

Whether netting fish, driving the boat, looking for fish or just reading water it's good to have a pair of polaroid glasses covering your eyes. They serve as protection from ultraviolet rays and stray hooks or weights. When running the river in a fast-moving boat even little raindrops or small gnats can feel like a bullet when they hit an unprotected eye. Polaroid glasses help us see fish, rocks and logs under water. They cut glare when trying to net a good fish and they make the day much more pleasant when you have to spend any part of it looking into the sun.

Most polaroids are expensive, so make sure you have a good glasses case to protect them. The case will also help keep them clean. Spending a few bucks for a strap to keep the glasses on your body instead of in the drink is also a wise investment.

"Hat Eyes" have been on the market for a few years. You'll see me wearing them in the DVD often because I fish in a rainy and misty environment and regular glasses just don't cut it. When your eyes no longer focus on close-up objects this invention really helps. The lenses are mounted under the bill of your ball cap with a clip. The whole operation stays dry under the bill and is instantly ready when you need to tie up a new rig or resolve a line tangle. Just a flip and they are in place and a push and they are up and out of the way. On a wet, foggy, breezy morning I can't see to get my leader into the eye of the hook without putting on glasses. With Hat Eyes it's an easy deal. They are available online and are one of the best things going for us older fishermen and women. AND they are very inexpensive!

CHAPTER X
Time

It waits for no one and, once spent, is irretrievable. You have made extensive preparations and are ready to hit the river. Will you spend your river time wisely?

You arose early, gulped down breakfast, drove too fast to the river and got to "The Hole" just in time to see another guy set the hook on your twelve-pound chromer. The question is begged, "Was your time used wisely?"

Johnny Rutherford said, "Luck is where preparation and perspiration meet."

You are probably going steelheading for recreation purposes, it's supposed to be a pleasurable experience. You probably aren't steelheading for the food, because that way the average cost for steelhead is over $300 per pound (think about it). I have some suggestions that will make the day much more pleasurable and drop the cost of that fish considerably.

Get Ready and Leave Early

Make sure you have all your gear. Get it together the night before. Place it in a corner out of the way where it is easily accessible to your vehicle. A checklist will help you remember ALL the things you want to bring; a permanent checklist is a great thing to make. Having the gear ready will save time in the morning and save frustration at a time when tension can set the wrong tone for the day. How many times have you forgotten your (fill in the blank) only to remember it five long miles down the road? Little things like lunch, bait and licenses are important and should be ready the night before and/or accompanied by a note on top of your pile of gear.

Why rush? Get up a few minutes early after going to bed a little earlier. If you are well rested and leave in plenty of time you will be the one getting first water. Allow time for traffic problems and slick, rainy roads. Allow time to get down to the river safely. One of the prettiest times of the day is just before it starts to get light. The world is awakening and as it does so it awakens your spirit. A few minutes spent looking at a drift will usually reveal things you won't see while fishing. Getting there early will reveal steelhead that are rolling. Often they will spend the low-light hours in one area only to move as the day breaks. Catching them yawning is **good**: They can't see the leader and they can't see you. The stealth approach works best under cover of low light.

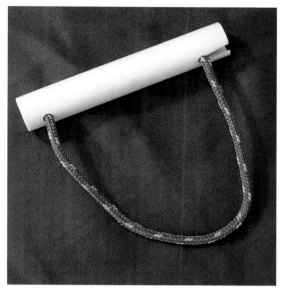

If you are taking a fish home this little carrier made from a piece of PVC and a length of braided nylon will make the long walk out a lot easier.

Be Prepared

You know where you're going and you know what you'll be using on the end of your line those first few casts. Why not have it tied on and ready to go? The best time of day is usually at first light, don't spend that time tying on equipment. Have your terminal tackle on the rod and ready to go. The rod can be carried broken down but ready; rubberbands work well for this. Velcro works even better and will not break. While your partner is fumbling in the gloom with water on his glasses you are making your first cast. While he was looking for his spool of lead you were watching that boil on the other side of the pool. While he was putting his rod together you were landing your first fish. You were prepared: You made your own luck by getting your gear together the night before and you were rewarded.

Belly boxes are a great invention; everything you need is on a belt and out of the way. When opened it makes a little work table and stays out of the way. The newer models have hinges that don't stand up to really cold temperatures so care must be taken not to stress them.

All that getting prepared can come to naught if you snag up on the third cast after landing that steelie. Bring a second rod that is also ready to go. That second rod can save your bacon if you get a little sand in the reel or manage to "birdie" it with an unseen tree branch. Instead of madly trying to unsnarl your bird's nest in the low light of morning, set the rod down, pick up your other one and continue the quest. Your partner just lost his rig on a snag and you just cast to a rising fish. **Wham!** That fish was hungry. Four casts and you are tagged out; your partner is not amused.

One of two things will now happen with your (possibly former) friend that helped you land that second fish. He too will be prepared on the next trip, or you may be fishing alone. To retain him as a sidekick you may want to refrain from gloating at this juncture. Imagine, however, the feelings you have versus the feelings he has. A little preparation went a long way toward making this one a day to remember—for both of you.

Time On the Water

Steelhead seldom attack offerings that are not in the water. Anything you can do to keep your line in the water will go toward adding minutes to your quality fishing time. That second rod is one of the best examples of a way to keep on fishing. When the bite is on and the fish are grabbing anything, you want to be in the water.

Pre-tied leaders conveniently stored in leader packs will add precious minutes to your day. These leaders work even better if the drifter and yarn are also attached. Tying up a complete set and getting back in the water will take close to five minutes. Tying on a prepared setup will take less than half a minute. If you lose a dozen rigs in a day you will give yourself almost an hour of additional "water time" by using pre-tied setups.

Sharp hooks are a must. Some people I know still use cheap hooks right out of the box without ever sharpening or even testing them for sharpness. Those pre-tied leaders should also be pre-sharpened and ready to go.

Time-saving Equipment

A vest is indispensable for maximizing your time on the water. You are hip deep in your favorite drift and lose a rig to a snag. Many people wade back to shore, sit down and tie up a new one. Yours are pre-tied, ready to go **and** you remain standing in the same place because you are wearing a vest. By the time the other guy has gotten over to his gear bag you are back in the water fishing. That roller on the other side of the drift has just taken your drifter and you are in for a battle while the other guy gets to watch. If you don't like the weight of a vest you can go for something as small as a fanny pack. If you think about it, you need very little in the way of gear. Keep it simple and on your body. You'll have much more water time.

Anything that will keep you from walking back to the bank will allow for more time in the water. It is unnecessary to carry a great deal of gear when you are actually fishing. A belly box or fanny pack that will provide access to a file, pair of pliers,

A vest is great but it gets heavy and wet in a hurry. These packs accommodate even your lunch and are a breeze to carry and get dried out.

a small assortment of drifters, weights and leaders will do. Berkeley makes a nice system for less than twenty dollars. It has its own belt and holds plenty of gear in compartments. It looks like a big belt buckle because it is hinged at the bottom. Hit the release and it flops down to reveal all your gear with a handy platform to work on. Fold it back up and you are ready to fish. Fanny packs perform the same function but the gear is not as well displayed. For just a few dollars you can add hours to your fishing trips by using anything that avoids a trip back to the bank after a break-off or landing a fish.

CHAPTER XI

Scents

Salmon and steelhead are able to circumnavigate the Pacific Ocean only to return to the native stream and gravel bed where they were hatched. They are able to do this primarily by their olfactory sense. If we compare noses to vision, humans are nearly blind, dogs see in black and white and steelhead smell in Technicolor. A good bloodhound is able to track for miles. Steelhead and salmon are able to do it over half the world. If their sense of smell is that good, might it not be used against them?

Picture this: You are walking down a busy street. You walk by a bakery where the doughnuts are just coming out of the fryer. The vent duct is strategically placed to catch your nose. The same tactic is used in movie theaters where the popcorn smell is allowed into the ducting system. Would you normally pay six bucks for a nickel's worth of corn and butter oil? Perfume placed gently on a well-turned nape has led many a good man down the aisle. If this technique works so well on nasally blind humans think of what it could to a steelhead.

Eggs, shrimp and sand shrimp all have a pleasing odor to steelhead because they are food items. All three are occasionally difficult to procure and usually expensive. All three are very productive baits that account for a significant percentage of steelhead that are caught.

Most baits that are presented are tuned to attract visually. In the murky waters of a winter-swollen stream this can be an iffy process. That is why adding a gob of eggs or a shrimp tail will often turn the trick when a plain Corkie produced no strikes. It is the scent in these baits that advertises a coming attraction to steelhead downstream. The scent allows a lethargic steelie to receive a heads-up before the bait arrives. It gets to smell the popcorn before the concession stand comes into view. Its appetite is whetted before the offering becomes available.

Bait oils and gels provide the same service without having to remember to go to the store to get the perishable shrimp

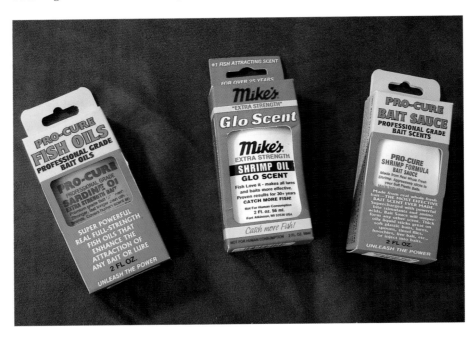

Steelhead and salmon smell in parts per billion. If we compare smelling to eyesight, humans are blind, dogs see in black and white while steelhead see in Technicolor. Why not use their best sense against them with a little chemical warfare?

or having to procure then cure eggs. A little dab of shrimp oil on a Corkie or some bait jelly applied to the back of a hotshot sends a message downstream that something good is coming their way. These oils are concentrated and will give off a scent superior in quantity to those exuded by natural baits. These oils and gels are preserved, however, and the quality of the scent may not match that of the natural offering.

Bait oils and scents can be mixed to entice steelhead with something new. Just because it's not a smell they are familiar with doesn't mean that it's a smell to which they would not be attracted. The same applies to men and perfume. It does not need to smell of food to be found attractive by the human animal!

Pheromones are new on the market. They are chemical messages released in air and water by many different animals to advertise availability to mate, territoriality or even fear. Pheromones have been shown to cause behavior in animals and humans that would not normally take place in the absence of the chemical. Baitfish exude a fear pheromone that tends to cause salmon and steelhead to go into a feeding frenzy. Capturing or replicating this substance and applying it to a bait offering will dramatically alter the steelhead's hesitation to bite.

The addition of a little yarn to the back of a drifter will substantially add to the surface area that will distribute the bait oil in the water. Slinkies provide an excellent distribution system while drift fishing. Simply apply the oil to the drifter, line and slinkie to increase the oil-impregnated surface area.

Scents attract steelhead to pick up the offering and mouth it but they seem to quickly determine it's not food and reject it. This is where that little bit of yarn and a sharp hook come into play. The yarn tends to catch in teeth and the sharp hook seals the deal. Scent will definitely get you more strikes and the fish is not likely to swallow the drifter. This makes the system an ideal offering for native fish or fish that will be released. For fish that will be kept it's hard to beat the real thing, shrimp or eggs on the hook.

One last thing to remember about scents—the key word is subtle. It seems we all had an eighty-year-old aunt that just loved perfume. I mean she **really** loved perfume! She always loved to give you a big hug and kiss before she gave you the present she brought. You loved the present but hated the hug. Too much scent is probably worse than none at all. Some scents, such as garlic and Ultrabite, are best served up in very small doses. A little goes a long way and the critters do have very sensitive noses. Just like Brylcream—"a little dab'll do ya"!

Another good tip when using scents is to start low in a drift (if possible) and work upstream. The reason for this is that fish above you will not have smelled the scent you are using at all if you progressively move and fish upstream. If you start high and proceed down they just keep getting a stronger dose before they eyeball the real goodies. If you

Spoon Scent Disbursion

Salmon and steelhead have some of the best noses in the animal world. Proper use of scents will dramatically increase the probability of a hookup when a lure or bait is put in front of that nose.

can, start low and end high in a pool or drift and save the surprise for an undiluted chemical attack.

Kludge, Goo and Spooge

Scent is a two-edged sword. The addition of scent to a lure package can dramatically increase OR decrease your chance of hooking fish. Steelhead have incredibly good noses that help them find prey but also keep them out of danger. That nose tells them of predators in the stream that would gladly treat them as a meal. It also tells them what is and isn't good to eat. If you are using scent, why not make sure you are using it to attract rather than repel.

An interesting science project is to take a rod with what you think is a clean handle and place it in a slightly

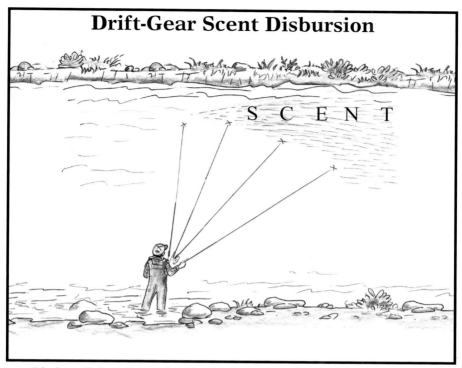

Drift-Gear Scent Disbursion

S C E N T

*Giving fish a "preview" of coming attractions before they
see your offering wakes them up and gets them in the mood.
Applying scent to a slinkie allows much more odor to be
distributed in the water. Adding scent to your
leader works the same way.*

moistened rod tube. Seal the tube and put it in a cool,
dark place for two weeks. When you open the case you
will immediately detect the pungent odor and notice the
handle is covered with spots and "fur". The mold, mildew
and bacteria that have grown on that "clean" handle have
created chemicals that would repel a great white.

I often see guides wearing latex or nitrile gloves to
prevent their hand odor from coming in contact with the
bait or lure. While wearing gloves, however, they grasp dirty
rods, tiller and oar handles, nets, tackle boxes, etc. The oars
have especially strong odors because guides work up a good
sweat rowing and every lick remains on the oars.

Ninety-five percent of the steelhead I land are on a drifter without yarn using only a scent and very seldom any bait. Using the right scent with whatever type of fishing you are doing exponentially increases your chance of a hookup.

Several of the guides that I use employ gloves for themselves and have their clients use commercial hand deodorizers throughout the day. Several drops of this liquid ensure that the bacon, cigar and after-shave odors are muted and rendered inert. These guides keep their boat surgically clean and their success rate reflects that effort. Their rod handles are cleaned at the end of the day. Bait boxes are washed and lures are carefully cleaned to remove any lingering scents or oils applied during the day's trip. The interior of the boat is carefully washed and all blood and slime is removed. Scent preparations that are used on the bait or lures are fresh and have been kept cool or refrigerated. If sardine-wrapped lures are used they were prepared the night before, kept in a cool place and the lures were washed with a detergent like Lemon Joy. They were allowed to thoroughly dry before wrapping. The sand shrimp keeper was also well scoured and the critters inside were handled with care to keep their particular perfume intact. Without care, that fish-enticing perfume can turn into a nightmare with the addition of a little warmth. Just let one of these critters get loose in your trunk and you'll see what a hungry steelhead smells when just a little is left in the bottom of the bait box.

One of the best examples for having fresh scents protected from heat and sun is the old standby, Dr. Juice. This elixir has caused me to catch hundreds of steelhead that would have remained streambound. BUT, if it spends too much time in the vest or in the boat it shrinks within the bottle and becomes dark and viscous. The enticing factors in this scent can become a repellant and repugnant to sensitive noses, both fish and human. Keep your scents and baits cool and protected and they will work much better for much longer.

When going from place to place in a boat keep lures and bait from touching surfaces. An egg gob dropped onto the deck of a boat can pick up all sorts of odors steelhead might find off-putting. If the boat hasn't been cleaned, the blood and slime from yesterday (or last month) are going to make an excellent repellant for those eggs you prepared with such love. Think of the bacterial load added to the bottom of a boat just by stepping ashore on any Tillamook stream. Those cows put out a lot more than sweet country milk!

CHAPTER XII
Casting and Catching

If you have to wind up like a surfcaster to get the offering to the drift you have the wrong equipment. A gentle flip of the arm and wrist should propel your bait to the right place without rocking others out of the boat or causing a 6.5 on the Richter Scale.

If finesse and distance are needed, why not use a light spinning reel with light line and a long rod with big eyes. This combination will set a lure flying almost a football field in length. You probably won't be able to set the hook as well but at least you got it over where you wanted it. There are some areas, however, that need a long cast. I have one **old** fiberglass rod with huge eyes and a Quick 220 reel that will put the lure 70 yards without much of a twitch. I use this rod in only one place and that place is usually good for a fish. I don't land many of them because there is about ten yards of stretch in the line but I do get the hits in that slot.

A properly tuned level-wind with the right line will provide me with almost as much distance but I have to throw a lot harder. The problem comes with overrun on the reel that results in backlashes. If I get a backlash on one of these casts it is usually a beauty. A real bird's nest develops when I manage to catch a branch or twig as I'm doing the hearty fling thing.

Most casts do not demand these heroic efforts, however, and a gentle cast properly done will save a lot of energy.

A properly balanced and adjusted level-wind will give excellent casts with a minimum of effort. To adjust line tension I hold the rod parallel with the ground and then release the line. It should come off the reel and drop steadily but not too rapidly to the ground. It should not over-run substantially on the spool once it has hit the ground. The outfit must have the right diameter of line on the reel. The rod must be limber enough to load well during a cast and the weight must be sufficient to propel the bait to the drift. This is now a balanced and tuned outfit.

One factor that many fishermen do not consider is lubrication of their reel. A well-oiled reel will perform at its optimum. One with too much or too heavy a lubricant will not work well at all. The lubricant that comes with most quality reels will usually work best under all but the most extreme conditions. In a pinch a small can of WD-40 will solve a multitude of problems and provide a good but temporary lubricant. Take time to make sure your reel is properly oiled before you have a problem on the river. Just in case have your reel's particular tool with you and the small container of the old WD. You never know when the WD-40 might act as a good scent. Many a fish has died after a sniff of that stuff.

Fishing Different Conditions

FISHING HIGH WATER

If I was given a choice between having to fish water that was too high or water that was too low I would take high water every time. In higher flows fish are still eager to bite as long as the river is stable, or better yet dropping. As long as there is not a danger posed by the high water, such as logs in the stream or bank erosion, there is no reason not to fish the rivers.

In high-water situations fish will be out of the main stream flow and behind obstacles that block the river's current or along the bank where the flow is less severe.

They are willing to bite and are active just trying to stay in one place. Leaves and debris flowing in the current will retard the bite so it might be best to wait until the river has flushed sufficiently. If the river is dropping, the amount of material in the water will quickly decrease unless heavy winds are adding to the problem with more leaves or needles. Sediment in the river usually decreases rapidly in a smaller falling river. I have begun fishing early in the morning and seen sand boiling out in the main current. In a few hours the silt decreases and the river loses its brown and swings to a beautiful steelhead green. If there are fish present this can be a golden time. It is not completely necessary to go to heavy gear, bigger weights and larger tackle. Often in these conditions the fish will be right next to the bank. A small drifter and

*The "Golden Time" on the Deschutes River with Jim Martin.
It's that very special time when the stars are gone and the sun
is on the hills but not the water. Jim's forgotten more than
most of us will ever know about steelhead.*

very little lead will get the offering to just the right place under the steelhead's nose. Larger drifters or even six-inch pink worms have a place in situations such as this. A bigger silhouette will help fish locate and take the drifter. Baits such as eggs, shrimp or even night crawlers work under these conditions and improve the chances of a take. If plugs are being pulled it's best to go to a larger body with a rattle and to use bright colors or black which will provide a good silhouette in murky water. Scents help fish locate drifters or plugs by advertising that something good is coming. Yarn on the back of the drifter will increase the lure's apparent size and help hold the scent longer and disburse it better. If you are in a situation where you do not have larger drifters there is a simple solution. Put two of the smaller ones on the leader. It's best if the selected drifters were of contrasting colors to make the offering even more visible and enticing.

FISHING LOW WATER

Rivers that are gin clear and low on water provide special challenges to fishermen. Usually, but not always, the best fishing will be very early in the morning and late in the evening. In most circumstances, once the sun has hit the water, the game is over. This may not be the case, however, if the water is cold or if the fish feel comfortable in a specific lie. No matter what, they will be spooky and difficult to approach successfully. You may only get one cast before you are busted so it is necessary to make it count. The stream must be approached carefully and quietly. Your footsteps and tripping over rocks at the water's edge may be detected by the fish. Coming to the river wearing your best orange hunting cap might be a mistake. Leaving your water-loving golden retriever at home is a smart move.

Polaroid glasses are a must in these conditions. Spotting the fish first gives you a huge edge. Stalk the fish and determine from where the best cast can be made. Notice the drift line and make sure your cast puts the lure in front of the fish on the first try. Scent on a drifter or jig helps when the water is low. Using a bobber to get just the right drift with a jig can work well under these conditions. The bobber allows you to get well upstream and float your bait down to the fish without being seen. The retrieve must be such that the bobber and bait don't spook the fish when you reel in. An assistant can be very helpful in this situation. He can tell you if your drift is in need of adjustment. The assistant can even let you know that the fish has taken the bait if the current is so slow the strike might go undetected.

Some states allow fishing all night on certain rivers and others allow fishing before sunrise and after sunset for a time. In low-water situations phosphorescent lures and jigs can be a killer option. The size of the hook and leader makes little difference because fish can't see them if it is dark. They can only see the lure and in the dark they are not at all hesitant to bite.

I have taken hundreds of summer steelhead on a single rig. This is a size 8 green glow in the dark Corkie with a 3/0 hook and a halogen flashlight to light up the drifter. Many people use a photo flash to illuminate the drifter but I have found that some of the flash may leak out and spook the fish. A small flashlight with a halogen bulb works very well for this task and the results can be spectacular.

In low, clear water fish lie in the tailout in the dark and don't move until the daylight disturbs them. Once you know where these fish are apt to lie you can shine up the drifter and cast to them using only the light of the lure to show you where the cast is going. The technique is deadly under the right circumstances, the two most important being darkness and fish.

Using scent to advertise the coming attraction to the fish can be very helpful when fishing in the dark. Changing scent can get fish that have been stung with a missed hookset to come back and try again. The yarn can allow more scent to be loaded on the lure but the yarn should not be below the point of the hook. Fish will be seeing the lure from the back and the yarn, which does not glow, makes it harder to see. Apply yarn above the drifter or use the "doublecross" configuration to retain visibility and still get the benefit of scent on the yarn. You need to get up early or stay late to make this work, but work it does. Make sure you know the regulations pertaining to this type of fishing and make sure you have your watch set to the exact time so you know when you must start or stop fishing.

FISHING IN THE WIND

Under most circumstances I would rather take a beating than have to fish in the wind. Nothing goes right, you can't control the boat, casts don't go where you aim, the river's full of leaves and branches and you can't feel the bites. Or can you?

Several techniques allow you to successfully catch steelhead in the wind. Three days before this was written I fished the upper Sandy River in wind gusts of nearly fifty miles per hour. I was drift fishing and managed to land two nice winter fish on nothing but a Corkie with scent. The wind was so strong that twice it blew my line completely out of the water and into the trees behind me. I did not want to fish in the wind but the water was right and the fish were there. I'm sure I had more bites than I was able to detect but two hatchery hens bit the dust even with the adverse conditions.

If the winds are steady and you can get above the area to be fished with the wind at your back you can stay in the game. A spoon works well in this situation. Get the spoon into the water and control the line by keeping the tip of the rod very close to the water. This gives the wind only a small purchase on the line that is above water. Casts can be interesting, but with the rod held low and pointed directly at the spoon on the retrieve you can feel the hits and take fish.

Drift fishing in the wind is more difficult. The use of a slinkie rather than lead allows bait to move along the bottom with enough weight to hold the line down in the water and not get snagged. Bait is a good addition when fishing in wind. Fish tend to hold on to the offering a little longer or even swallow the bait making the catch a sure thing.

Casting can be very difficult while drift fishing in high winds. It becomes necessary to use a heavier weight just to get the cast to go where you want. When you cast, try to wait

Kids are like steelhead...Best when hooked early!

for a lull in the gale. Cast hard and then at the end of the cast, before your bait hits the water, stop the line. The wind will have pulled a big belly in your line and putting on the brakes while casting will reduce this belly. Quickly drop the tip of your rod to the water and reel-in any excess line. Keep the rod very low to the water and keep the rod pointed at the bait. It may be necessary to reel up a little line occasionally but you will be fishing. Use the low-rodding technique to stay in touch with the bait. Fishing in the wind is no fun but it beats not fishing at all. Besides, you'll probably have the place all to yourself.

FISHING VS. CATCHING

It's said that ten percent of fishermen catch 90 percent of fish. In steelheading this is definitely a true statement. If you are taking the time to read this book you may already fall into category two: "catchers". Many people like to go to Las Vegas to gamble, catchers go to Vegas to WIN!

Category one fishermen hit the river several times a year carrying a tackle box and show up on the bank about 9:00 AM. They are there on a Saturday or Sunday morning and have made little or no preparation. It is these folks that the departments of fish and wildlife rely upon to pay for the steelhead you catch. They are mostly good folks with good intentions but a small portion of them are the slob fishermen that we have all seen.

Category two fishermen have done their homework and know fish are in the river. They have equipment appropriate to the job at hand and they show up at a time when there are few fishermen and plenty of fish. They have come to the river to mine its bounty and are serious about the task. A game plan was laid and the exact terminal tackle needed is pre-tied in quantity to account for the ever-present snags. The first three casts usually yield a fish and the tone for the day is set. The fish is quickly and quietly fought to the bank and gently released or dispatched for the table. The leader is changed, knots checked and the process begins again. To catchers, steelheading is not a matter of life or death. To them it is much more important than mere mortality. Like any fanatic, they eat, breathe and drink steelheading. Their spouses are hesitant to take them to a party because they will corner some little old lady and expound upon their most recent egg cure discovery. Speaking of spouses, God help the one that washes that vest. The thing lay in the back of the pickup all winter and the dog may have given birth on it, but it cannot be sullied in the washer. When a vest is ready, it, like the flag, must be ceremonially burned—but never washed. Sounds like a fishing fanatic, doesn't it?

Steelhead are a rare commodity. They are called the fish of a thousand casts for a reason. True catchers pay the price in money, family and friends to become one of the elite, one of the "One Percenters". They are the True Believers of steelheaders. They are on the river at legal time in the

Free Fishing Day at Hagg Lake near Forest Grove, Oregon.
These future rafters will remember this day fondly
for all their lives.

mornings. They show up at Game Commission meetings to fight for the rights of all steelheaders. They join groups that build and maintain river facilities for all fishermen. They pay hard-earned dollars to special interest groups and lobbyists to assure steelhead, salmon and the environment are preserved for generations yet unborn. Without these folks many of our rivers would have been closed and hatchery programs laid to rest. Loggers would have laid waste to the forest, and streams would run mud with every winter rain. A few rivers would contain even fewer wild fish available to elitists who would restrict access to themselves.

The "One Percenters" are the pointy end of the stick that jabs at those who would allow steelheading to become a game played by only a few. It is not necessary to become one to be good at catching steelies. It IS necessary to provide them and their organizations support to make sure their work is carried on and the fish and the environment are protected. Folks that catch a lot of steelhead, obviously, do not keep them all or their tags would be filled in a couple of good weeks. That means they release most, if not all, of their fish.

Many times I've seen steelhead and salmon that are going to be released drug up on a bank, bashed around on the rocks, man-handled in a net, then let go with the possibility they might live. Some are even grabbed under the gill and held up for others to admire. They might live but will likely develop fungus due to the removal of their slime layer. This means they might spawn but will most likely die and not return in another year six or seven pounds heavier.

When handling a large fish that is going to be released treat it as gently as you would a human baby. Both are very delicate. Cradle it carefully and don't use a net if at all possible. Try not to let the fish thrash on the shore. This can damage their skin and will not be good for the eyes or gills. Barbless hooks work wonders for releasing fish. They actually penetrate better on the hookset than a barbed hook and hold well if you keep even tension on the line when the fish is running or jumping. If a picture is needed, keep the fish in the water. Carefully support the fish with both hands while the picture is being shot, then make sure it is ready to swim away before releasing it. These fish are a valuable resource and the parents of future generations. Protect the resource and enjoy the rewards years from now.

CHAPTER XIII
Logs and Records

Maintaining a Log

If you are 94 years old with a photographic memory you don't need to read this. If you are not, pay special attention. Those who do not study history are doomed to repeat it. When you are on the river you are making history. Techniques, baits and tackle that worked under certain conditions in 1984 will probably still work today—under the same conditions.

My own logs go back over a quarter century. The information is invaluable for planning trips and determining what tackle and technique to use. On cold, rainy nights when the rivers are out it is enjoyable to sit down and go back all those years to see what I was doing, where I was going and what was working. This helps to figure out what to tie up in preparation for lower water and nicer days.

The log can be kept on a computer or just recorded in a spiral notebook. The method is not nearly as important as the fact that the information is kept in some form.

Here are the items I have found most useful:
- Place: The name of the lake, river, bay or stream. This information not only includes the basic area but the exact location(s). This can even be broken down to certain pools, drifts or any body of water. Have you ever been anchored up and the boat next to you is killing them while you are biteless? That boat's location, properly recorded, can get you into the proper spot next year, next week or tomorrow. Recording the place and specific location can be extremely important and is the most basic fact in the log.
- Date: Obvious.
- Technique: What type of fishing were you doing? In the same area you may be drift fishing one day and bobber or boondogging on another. Other factors will determine what works best, but make sure to record the basics before you get to the specific.

•Tackle: The more information you record the better. Very specific information on what was working and what wasn't will make or break future trips. Recording the exact size of the drifter, color of yarn, fly pattern, finish on the plug, type of scent used will tell you in future years what worked on these fish. Information on what others used also allows you to be more properly equipped, assuming they did well. It's just as important to record what was not working so as to avoid spending time on the river with unproductive tackle.

•River Conditions: These can vary widely from day to day, or even hour to hour. If at all possible, record the exact river height at the time you were fishing. This information is available in the paper, by phone or online. It is probably the most important statistic for planning your trip as your technique and tackle will primarily be determined by this one feature. Record if the river was rising, falling or stable. Steelies react very differently on rising versus falling water, make sure this information is there.

•Water clarity: This will help you get a feel for the water at certain levels. Your favorite river will probably be an entirely different color if two feet of water are added. If you record water clarity it will help you remember what particular colors and sizes of tackle to use on future trips.

•Weather conditions: These are very important as well. The water may be perfect but that lower river is a terror in an east wind. Fishing the protected upper river in the same wind can yield a great trip. That one little piece of information can make or break future trips. Cloudy days are usually better fishing than those with full sun. All other conditions can be perfect but full sun will usually send fish to deeper pools or broken water. Steelhead do not have eyelids so they do not get to squint in bright sunlight. Fishing broken water or deep pools will yield fish on some days but not others. Fishing the right places under the right conditions will cut in half the areas of the river you need to hit, and improve your chances of success. Rain, snow and air temperature affect water temperature. Steelies are exothermic and their metabolic activity is completely determined by water temperature. Water and air temperature, then, are also extremely important. Oxygen levels are determined by water temperature and flow. Warm, sunny days with low water usually produce lethargic fish. You might wish to adjust the time you fish to get the water with the highest oxygen content and the lowest temperature. Cold winter days work just the opposite. A rise of two degrees in the water temp will spur a bite in the afternoon when the water temperature is highest and fish are laying in bright sun.

• Time of Day: The norm for steelhead is early morning and late afternoon or evening will produce the best chances of encountering a biter. Recording the time fish were taken or even when the bites occurred will give you important information, telling you if you have to arise at 3:00 AM or if you can stop for a leisurely breakfast. This information can tell you to take off work two hours early for the evening bite. Using up two hours of vacation time rather than a whole day gives you four times as many fishing trips because you are hitting the river at prime time and on an uncrowded weekday. Many times, for no apparent reason, a bite will occur on a river at a specific time. After thirty-plus years of fishing the Sandy River I know that I need to be alert at 10 AM. The ten o'clock bite works the same on that river in winter or spring. It does not appear to have any connection to anything but time. Those Sandy steelies just need to chew on something at ten!

Other information that can be important to record would be anything that affects the fishes' movement or willingness to bite. Tides, number of people fishing, number of boats on the river, how others faired, leaves in the river—anything that affects the fish—write it down. It doesn't take too many years of recording these factors before patterns begin to develop. If you know the fish are there, the water, weather and time of day are right and that pink pearl corkies with a bit of egg worked for the last three years, then you have a move to make—now!

The only way to get this information is to start recording. Once you have a log you may (or may not) wish to share it with

Fishing Log

WATER:	COMPANION:		DATE:	TIME:
WEATHER:	AIR TEMP:	WATER TEMP:		BAROMETER:
WATER CONDITION:		WIND:	TIDE:	MOON:

FISHING EQUIPMENT:

FLIES/LURES:

HATCHES/OTHER FOODS/FEEDING ACTIVITY:

SPECIES: HOOKED: LANDED: RELEASED: LARGEST: KEPT:

TRIP OBSERVATIONS:

TIME	SIZE	SPECIES	SPECIAL FISH SIZE & NAME OF FLY OR OTHER OFFERING	STRETCH

very close friends. This can work into a situation of 'you show me yours and I'll show you mine'. The more information you have the better the chances you'll be at the right place at the right time doing the right thing with the right gear and bait.

Photos and Videos

You must remember how some formerly good friends invited you over for dinner and you had to sit through their slide show about their trip to the Grand Canyon. This is your chance for payback. For very little money you can get 35mm cameras that are disposable, waterproof, dustproof, slimeproof and will even stand up to egg spooge (that pink stuff all over everything). Camcorders are now under three hundred bucks. With a little care they will stand up to a trip down the bank in a padded pack and enclosed in a one-gallon zip-lock freezer bag. Recording

Waterproof and water-resistant cameras are a must. The cost on these run from less than a hundred dollars to about two hundred. The top model is a full dive camera, the middle and bottom ones are only water resistant. All produce excellent pictures and stand up well to a wetting.

your information in a log allows you to recall events, but taking pictures or videos allows you to relive them.

The hard thing about having a camera along is remembering to use it. It's nice to have a picture at the end of the day holding up that pair of fish you landed on the Suckaguamish River. By the end of the day, though, the fish may be discolored, bent and quite unpleasing to the eye. A video of this same scene is even worse. Here are some ideas about how to improve these pictures. We'll start at the end of the day and work backwards.

The "mighty hunter" pic at the end of the day can be improved without too much work. Here are a few suggestions:

- Always use a flash. The pictures at the end of the ride will usually be in lower light or will have a bright background. The "fill in flash" will brighten the foreground, you and the fish.
- Have the folks holding the fish remove their sunglasses and tip back the bills on their caps so you can see who they are.
- Turn the fish so the sides are perpendicular to the camera. Otherwise you get a great silhouette of a fish and two pectoral fins.
- If the fish is bent from resting in the bottom of something, straighten it out. Get all the blood off the fish and take the picture before the fish has been cleaned.
- Tell the shooter to push the button slowly. Inexpensive cameras have a very slow shutter speed and this will prevent blurring.
- Take one picture with the camera held vertically and one horizontally.
- Provide an interesting background, the river, the driftboat, mountains or maybe a waterfall.
- If you take just a few seconds to prepare a shot, it may just be something you'd like to have blown up and hung on a wall. Use the camera during the day's fishing. Sunrises, fog on the water, waterfalls, fish being fought or fish being landed are great topics for taking a picture. Some disposable cameras come in underwater varieties and can give very interesting pictures of fish being brought to the boat.

- Videography is another matter entirely when it comes to shooting. The tape is fully erasable and any mistakes will be without cost. Editing with videotape is really easy as long as your VCR will "PAUSE" while recording. This pause will allow for seamless editing and makes for great stuff to show those friends who bored you with their slides. Put two VCR's together and you can even send a copy of the tape home with them for their future enjoyment! That's really paying them back.
- There are two problems with taking camcorders on a fishing trip: One grain of sand will completely incapacitate a camcorder and they do not handle moisture well. This problem is solved by keeping the camera in a one-gallon zip-lock bag or dry bag. Bring the camera out when you are going to use it and then IMMEDIATELY put it away.

Here are some hints that will make for excellent videos the first time out:

- Think about what you'd like to have on the finished tape and then remember to shoot it during the day.
- Walking into the pool to be fished or launching the driftboat are great scenes to set the tone of the day.
- Get some opening shots of the people on the trip rigging up rods or putting out lines. Remember, this thing records voices so tell the place and date of the trip and ask the participants to watch the "pottymouth" talk.
- You may actually catch a fish and you will want to be in the video. Plan ahead and teach one of the others how to turn on the camcorder and how to push the RECORD button. They need to know which end of the camera to point at you. (Yes, this really does happen—a lot.)
- An inexpensive camera may not have stabilization as a feature. Try to hold the camera still so it doesn't look like you're dancing while shooting the scene. Make sure the person shooting you knows this as well.
- Pan slowly from scene to scene. This will avoid motion sickness for the eventual viewers of the finished product. Try not to use the ZOOM feature too much.
- If a shot did not go well, ask the participants to redo it,

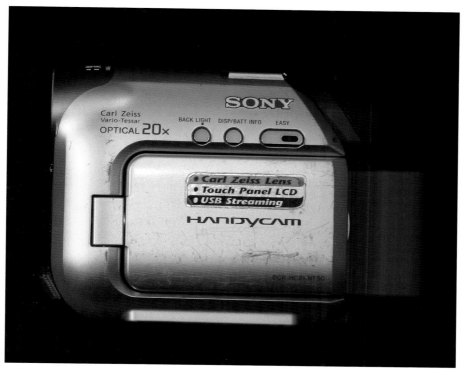

This Sony Handycam costs about $250 and has a high-capacity battery to last through days of videoing. As you can see by the scratches, this one has been through the mill but they are tough as a Timex watch. This one spends a lot of time in an underwater case that cost about $150 and makes the camera pretty much immune to anything but shock from a drop.

if possible. The bad shot can be edited out. This can be difficult to do if a hot bite is going on.

- Take lots of background video. This will make good filler for the finished tape and let others see the beauty of the area you visited.
- Before editing the tape, go through it first and make a list of the portions you want to permanently record. You do not need to record them to the VCR tape in order of taping. This mandates a preview and will greatly simplify making the finished and edited tape.
- Make sure your battery is fully charged and then get the camera out and use it!

CHAPTER XIV
Courtesy

Most people were brought up to be courteous and respectful. They were taught not to throw their clothes on the floor and to pick up after themselves. When they went to visit they were reminded to be especially watchful of their manners. Much of what was learned as a child failed to stick with a lot of folks. This is evidenced by the trash left at popular spots on riverbanks, tires and sofas deposited in urban rivers and cigarette butts everywhere.

The Golden Rule applies now more than ever. There are more of us using the outdoors and fewer of us caring about our impact on the earth. What you learned in kindergarten is still applicable:

- Don't crowd in line. The people ahead of you on the river got there first. Wait your turn or get up earlier and be at the head of the line next time. This applies at boat launches as well. Keep your place in line but be ready to put it in the water when your turn comes.
- There isn't always room for one more. If the hole is taken, wait your turn at the water or move on. If you insist on joining the lineup, do so quietly and with all due courtesy. Ask if you might join the group, maybe even schmooze a little. If your presence is clearly not wanted, pick another spot.
- Don't camp on a good piece of water. Get there early, give it your best shot and then move on. My dad's words were, "take some, leave some."
- If you brought it in, pack it out and maybe take a little extra junk out that those before you have forgotten. Take a garbage bag in the boat or in your pack. Make it a point to fill it up.
- Learn how to "field strip" a butt then please show others.
- In some states it is against the law to clean fish in bodies of water. This may be a poor rule because it removes vital nutrients from the stream BUT it keeps boat launches from looking like a slaughterhouse. Let common sense prevail.

If someone is playing a fish near you, it's always a good idea to reel in your line and wait until the person playing the fish is well out of your casting area.

*Sometimes there is room for one more! Here's a group of
Northwest Steelheaders repairing a boat slide on a
coastal river in Oregon. Many hands make light work
because moving those timbers and packing bags
of concrete down from the road is not an easy job.*

- If you are lucky enough to get "first water" and others are behind, you might consider staying well ahead of the pack or letting others go around. It is not good manners to jump to the next hole whenever another boat comes into sight.
- If someone is kind enough to take you out in their boat, provide the bait, row all day and drive you home, at least buy them dinner and a tank of gas. They may say it isn't necessary but make sure to at least offer. Ask if you can help clean the boat, clean the fish, or whatever—but ask!

CHAPTER XV
Boats

The definition of a boat is a hole in the water you keep trying to fill with money. That definition does not have to apply! There are ways around spending an arm and a leg to get down the river. If you want to go back up river—now that's gonna get expensive.

If you want to start by spending big bucks, buy a drift boat. A basic new one will run you about four grand, and fully loaded they are about six. There are some things to look for in a better drift boat. One of the most important things is to make sure the selected hull tracks well in the current, both while being rowed and at anchor. In a sixteen-foot model this usually requires a 54" beam at the bottom. This will keep the boat on a steady line and discourage it from sloughing back and forth at anchor. Another item

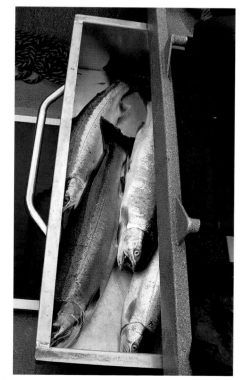

that allows the boat to track well at anchor is an offset anchor bracket. If the bracket is mounted off the centerline of the boat it will cause the craft to sit slightly sideways in the current. This discourages sloughing and allows a motor to be mounted on the transom and still have a stern anchor bracket.

Another item that allows for straight tracking at anchor

The results of a fine winter morning on Oregon's Wilson River using the doublecross and scent while fishing from a driftboat.

On a cold, wet winter's day nothing warms like a good propane heater. Just be careful to keep rain gear well away from the grill and element.

is "OarRights". These devices attach to the shaft of oars and cause the blades to stand vertically in the water when the oars are at ease. The blades naturally want to lie flat on the water but these devices help the oar blades to act as rudders that align the boat to the current.

A built-in fish box is an excellent item on the wish list. One can keep a nice chinook or steelie in a burlap sack in the bottom of the boat but they sure can get in the way at the worst possible time. A fish box mounted under the rower's seat allows for safe and effective storage of the bodies until the end of the day.

A third oar is an essential item only if you break or lose one of the other two. It's kind of like having a spare tire. You won't have a flat if you have the spare, but if you don't...

OarRights keep the oars angled vertically into the water for immediate action and serve to steady the boat at anchor and eliminate sloughing in current.

In the long run, extra money you spend on a galvanized trailer will come back to you. If the boat is used on days when gravel has been applied to the roads, a painted trailer will take a beating. Zinc prevents pitting from gravel hits and preserves the life of the trailer to match that of the boat. If you have a nice paint job and want to keep it that way, a boat bra will do the trick. The first trip for my new drift boat was on the Wilson on a frosty morning. The sanding crews had been busy the night before. When I got the boat to the put-in it looked like someone had taken a shotgun to the paint. Half a bottle of touch-up paint and a boat bra later the problem was solved and has never returned.

Money spent on quality, balanced oars make the days on the river go much faster. Oars that are not properly balanced are not a problem if you are used to rowing all day, every day. For the weekend warrior, however, quality, balanced oars are essential.

Aluminum and sharp rocks do not mix well. A drift boat passing over volcanic rocks will stop in the space of two inches, propelling its occupants forward dramatically. Before the boat hits the water, a good coat of plastic on the bottom will prevent fishermen from being launched like torpedoes from a PT boat when rocks are encountered.

Please, please, please, wear personal flotation gear. This year has been an all-time record for drownings in the

Even if you don't have a bad back, an anchor with a pulley works very well as long as you are not setting the anchor in deep water. With the same effort you can lift twice the weight with the pulley, but you have to hoist twice the length of line. It's a good tradeoff.

A piece of one-inch PVC pipe run from gunwale to gunwale with a rod caddy attached will keep the net out of the anchor line and the rods from fouling with each other.

Northwest. Hot summer days and cool water is always a bad mix for the unwary, occasional or intoxicated swimmer. You, however, know that you are entering a hazardous environment. A jet-boat trip up a large river in winter or a run down a small stream in a drift boat can yield the same result. One small slip and you are in the water. Coats, heavily-laden vests and boots guarantee that swimming will be almost impossible. If you look in almost any fishing catalogue you will find inflatable flotation devices that will get you out of trouble. Vests like the SOSuspenders are the best; they inflate instantaneously and keep you afloat indefinitely. The inflatable belts are completely out of the way and will get you out of trouble with a simple pull of the lanyard.

When I go on ANY boat I always wear my float coat or the suspenders. Others may think you look like a dork with the PFD—but... Here's a quick story: Two years ago I was on a licensed charter boat out of Sitka, Alaska. It had been inspected by the Coast Guard and had all the stickers prominently displayed. The skipper was newly hired and it was his first day on the boat. A long way off shore and with choppy seas that had built to six feet we decided to head in. The boat didn't feel right when he gave it the gas and I looked aft. There were six inches of water and fuel on the deck near the engine housing. The water flooding the bilge had shorted out the electronics (including the radio and the GPS) and the bilge pump wasn't hooked up. While he was fighting the boat I went looking for the life jackets. There weren't any! If that boat went down I knew I was going to become really popular since I had on the only flotation aboard other than a small ice chest. I'll let you figure out what I was going to do if the boat slipped beneath the waves; I did not plan to be part of the group. A good PFD will allow you to save yourself. It will also give you enough capability to get yourself out of trouble and maybe help others. Over the years I've pulled five people out of rivers and lakes that would not have made it out alive. I'm sixty years old and I'm not too sure I can do that again. Wearing a PFD, it's a cinch.

*Here's a better look at the full length of PVC
and how it's mounted.*

*The amount of damage an
unsecured 30-pound anchor can
do in just a few minutes on a
rough road is amazing. Always
properly stow and secure this
device.*

*A good bow anchor can save
the day when you encounter
a stiff upriver wind or lose
your main anchor.*

A tongue wheel will save your back and make hitching-up a breeze.

My first trip with this boat made the new paint look like it had been hit with a shotgun. The freshly graveled and sanded roads tore into the paint pretty badly. The bra on the boat solved that problem and has kept the boat looking new for years.

Pontoon Rafts

For very little money you can buy a lot of fun when you purchase a pontoon raft. A few years back these things sold for 700-800 bucks but now are down to under three hundred for a decent-quality boat. Common pontoon boats are 8 feet in length. Some of the larger ones will accommodate two people with tandem seating. The beauty of one-man boats is that they deflate and disassemble into a package about the size of a suitcase. They will fit under a bed, and two of them only take up part of a car's trunk. You can throw them over a guardrail and into a river and they come back up a bank with equal ease. You can get into areas that jet sleds and drift boats only dream about, and hit water that only the landowners get to see. Caution is definitely needed with these devices because the covering on the pontoons is only several thousandths of an inch thick and a stick or piece of metal can definitely wreck your whole day. Sweeper logs, underwater limbs and trunks can also be real dangers. You should always be wearing flotation on any boat, but these make it mandatory. Like diving, employ the buddy system when you're on the water in these little sport models.

All that being said, I can tell you I own two of them for a reason—they are a blast. If you are on a gentle stream on a summer's day don't worry about waders. If you are on a river with rapids in the dead of winter, thermal and wetness protection are paramount concerns. Chest waders keep the water out up to your waist but if you go through big rollers you're going to get really wet and cold. A good rain jacket that is tight around your middle and at the sleeves will make your day on the water much more enjoyable and comfortable.

Modifications and Additions

OarRights are mandatory in a pontoon. When you grab for the oars or are sitting at anchor you want to have the oar blades in the water vertically all the time. This makes the oars immediately accessible for fast maneuvering off the anchor and they keep the boat oriented in the current in moving water.

Flippers are necessary if you plan to fish from the boat. You need both hands to row and at least one hand to hold the rod. Battling a good-sized fish while trying to row to shore poses several problems. A set of easily removed flippers like you would use in a float tube will make the entire process end much better. Walking on a gravel beach or on river rocks is difficult while wearing flippers so they should be easily removable with the flip of a buckle. Wearing flippers that can be removed by just popping a little lever with one hand allows you to go over rocks, roots and limbs to run down that big chromer headed back to the big water.

Rod lanyards are also a necessity in a pontoon boat. If you drop a rod in a boat it will still be there to pick up. In a pontoon raft all you'll see is the handle sinking out of sight. They cost less than ten dollars and will help avoid a costly mistake if you slip. On occasion you might get a suicide bite from a big one and the lanyard will allow you and the fish to stay in touch if it pulls the rod from your cold wet hand.

A rod holder can be bought to add on to most pontoon boats, but one is just as easily made from ABS pipe. ABS comes in all shapes and sizes but 1 1/2 inch is just right for holding a rod. The rod holder can usually be attached to the bracket that holds your seat in place, or it can be placed on the side bar near the oar lock. A holder placed just in front of and below the seat will allow quick access and be out of the way of your oars. If you like to travel the river using two rods there is a simple solution for keeping the second rod out of harm's way. By using a little Velcro you can attach a one-foot-long piece of ABS pipe to the frame to hold the rod so that it points to the rear when you are going through rapids or under overhanging trees. You just have to remember you have a long tail when maneuvering the boat close to branches or shore.

Most pontoon boats now have anchor systems, but they are usually located in the middle of the craft behind the seat. This causes the boat to slough back and forth in the current. Using the factory anchor system you can place the anchor at the stern of the boat by adding a pulley. Most pontoons have a "D" ring at the aft end. Run a piece of 1/4-inch nylon line from one side to the other and knot off a pulley in the middle for the anchor line. The pulley and the OarRights will keep the boat very stable under all but the fastest water conditions.

Hard anchors or lead anchors do not work well in rocky or brushy conditions. They tend to foul at the worst possible time and are often lost. Instead of an anchor try using old tire chains. They hold the bottom really well and are difficult to get tangled to the point where they are lost. Another trick is to attach the anchor line to the chains with a piece of copper wire. The copper should be sturdy enough

*Going downriver in a driftboat or pontoon raft is a fairly
inexpensive process. If you want to go back upriver,
it's going to cost you a lot more money.*

that it will hold the boat but small enough in diameter that
a really hard jerk will break the wire and save your anchor
line which would have been sacrificed otherwise. A fouled
anchor in a pontoon boat can be serious because of the lack
of mobility while on the water. It's nearly impossible to row
upstream and get the anchor loose at the same time.

The very first fish I hooked in my boat was a chinook
about 35 pounds. It's still unclear which one of us had
the other on the line. That fish dragged me all over the
pool. Earlier I had made an agreement with my friends in
the drift boat that they would help me land any big fish I
hooked. They got a fish on and that agreement went out the
window. Our friendship was sorely tested by their laughter
at seeing me holding a large salmon grasped firmly between
my legs while trying to stay in the boat. It was then that I
invested in flippers. You can't "out-flipper" a big salmon,
but you can get yourself to shore and make the battle a
little more equal!

CHAPTER XVI
Playing Fish

Catch-and-release fishing for steelhead is heartily encouraged. Your release gives other anglers the opportunity to enjoy the antics of the same fish, and it allows the critter to go make babies. Some fish, however, should be killed. Hatchery fish that are not of native stock to the stream are stocked with the specific intent that they be taken for food. Allowing these fish to spawn with native stock dilutes the gene pool specific to that particular basin and current thinking is that these non-native fish should be killed.

So, now you've hooked a big one and it has decided to return to the ocean. Your reel spool is looking pretty bare and you can't follow it downstream any more. What are you going to do?

One trick that has saved my bacon on many occasions and worked every time except one (see the DVD) is to put the rod tip in the water as the fish is running downstream. I don't exactly know why this works but I know that it does. Lowering the angle of the pull seems to slow the fish down and eventually they will turn and face into the current. If it's a really big fish there is another trick that can be used. If there is any line left on the reel, feed it out. Yup, I mean slack line 'em. This puts the line next to the fish and the pull on the line is now coming from down river instead of up stream. When the fish takes off again it will be resisting the line and will swim upriver. This is to be encouraged: If you keep enough slack in the line the fish will eventually swim upstream and even past you. Once the fish has returned to your vicinity it's a good bet they will not swim downstream again. The fish tried this once and it didn't work, plus it will be tired from the fight, and then swim back upstream. Chances are really good that this fish will be landed.

When a fish gets close to the boat you must be very careful that the line does not touch anything. Steelhead lines are usually pretty small in diameter and easily parted.

If the fish goes under the boat, simply put the rod tip in the water and allow the fish to maneuver. Follow the fish around the boat, missing the anchor line, and fight them on the other side. If the fish is to be released, get them to the side of the boat and remove the hook, if possible. If the hook is too deep, cut the line and allow the fish to dispose of it on its own.

If you are fishing from the bank and the sand or rocks are not sharp, slide the fish onto the bank and let it go or keep it for a great dinner. Getting the fish onto the bank and keeping it there is pretty simple as long as it is well hooked. Play the fish until it comes to the bank willingly. Keep the rod very low to the bank and when the fish is going the right direction pull the fish to the bank with a sidearm motion. If you have help, your assistant can retain or release the fish but keep the pressure on the fish and keep the head pointed up the bank.

If I'm going to retain a fish I'll usually use a net whether I'm ashore or on the bank. I have a folding net that collapses into a pretty small package for bank work and I like to use a fairly large net for the boat. All my nets are black on both the frame and the bag. I have found that fish usually dive toward a black net, but tend to avoid a green mesh.

CHAPTER XVII
What to Do with your Fish

Filleting

To be able to easily fillet a salmon, trout or steelhead the fish must have been killed properly and kept preserved under acceptable conditions. One of the most important things to do when a fish is retained is to bleed it. After bonking it and while the heart is still beating, break or cut a gill and let it bleed out. The fish should be kept in a cool place laid flat and kept moist.

Lay the carcass out on a flat surface about the height of your elbow. Scrape the slime from the skin with the edge of a knife held perpendicularly to the body and then wash the slime from the surface of the fish and filleting board. Make the first cut behind the gills starting from the spine and going to just behind the pectoral fin. This cut should be to the bone but should not cut into any eggs when the visceral cavity is entered. Turn the fish so the dorsal fin is pointing toward you. Begin cutting along the spine at the same point you initially started with the knife held flat. Allow the blade to ride along the spine and cut the length of the fish, carefully separating the flesh from the bone by making small, slicing cuts. This will keep the fillet in one piece and not cause a bunch of flaps of flesh. Cut with one hand and pull the flesh back with the other to keep the spine and bones in view. Let the blade slide along the rib cage while gently lifting the meat and very little will be left on the carcass. Cut all the way to the belly meat and expose the one whole side. When this side is finished make the final cut by plunging the knife through the flesh just behind the vent and in front of the ventral fin. This fin and its muscles should be left on the carcass. Turn the fish to the other side and repeat the process. The resulting fillet can be kept whole or cut in half length-wise and then cut into chunks. The meat should be washed again and lightly dried. The best and easiest method of preserving is to vacuum

A good fillet knife is worth its weight in gold. The best knife, however, is only as good as the tools used to sharpen it. The hand sharpeners can keep you in business at the cleaning table but a good edge needs to be done slowly and carefully with good ceramic or flat stones.

Battling a nice hatchery buck at the North Fork of the Nehalem River Disabled Fishing Access.

The Association of Northwest Steelheaders donates over 30,000 hours of volunteer labor each year to assure that Oregon's fisheries are maintained for now and the future.

worked for Oregon Department of Fish and Wildlife and he knew this river inside out. I attended another chapter meeting at Steelheaders and joined up. Since then I've joined Tillamook Anglers, National Wildlife Federation, Common Waters and Trout Unlimited. My first love is still the best, however, and I am the current President of the Association of Northwest Steelheaders. The guy that got me interested is still helping me out and is still involved with STEP as a chapter chairman. All these organizations do good work for wildlife and for future generations who will want to enjoy the outdoors. You are reading this book because you have an interest in a magnificent sport. When compared to runs that existed before this country was settled, the few fish that remain, are a travesty. The reason they remain is that service and conservation organizations serve as the pointy end of the spear to goad and cajole decision makers into making the correct decisions for generations of people and wildlife yet unborn. You are a consumer of the work that was done by those that came before you. You, in turn, have an obligation to "pay it forward" so that those yet to come will have a chance to thrive and prosper in an unspoiled environment. Spend a few bucks and devote a few hours to join a worthy group. I found it to be a life-changing event.

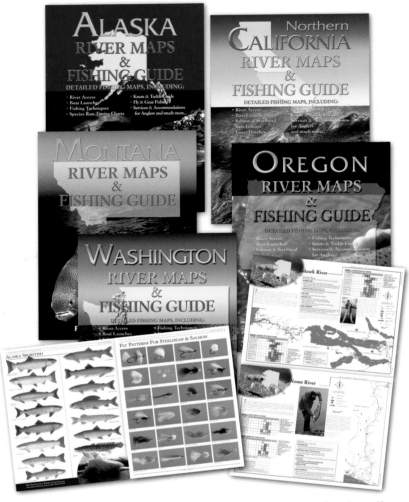

Learn from the Experts!

One year (10 big issues) for only $29.95!

Great Fishing Books!

JIG-FISHING FOR SALMON & STEELHEAD
by Dave Vedder

8 1/2 x 11 inches, 96 pages.
SB: $24.95
ISBN-13: 978-1-57188-391-9
UPC: 0-81127-00225-2

300 TIPS TO MORE SALMON & STEELHEAD
by Scott Haugen

8 1/2 x 11 inches, 136 pages.
SB: $29.95
ISBN-13: 978-1-57188-409-2
UPC: 0-81127-00243-6

SPOON FISHING FOR STEELHEAD
by Bill Herzog

8 1/2 x 11 inches, 64 pages.
SB: $14.95
ISBN-13: 978-1-878175-30-4
UPC: 0-66066-00119-1

ILLUSTRATED RIGGING FOR SALMON • STEELHEAD • TROUT
by Robert Campbell

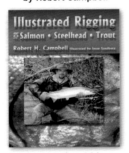

8 1/2 x 11 inches, 144 pages
SB: $29.95
ISBN-13: 978-1-57188-397-1
UPC: 0-81127-00231-3

SPINNER FISHING FOR STEELHEAD, SALMON AND TROUT
by Jed Davis

8 1/2 x 11 inches, 97 pages.
SB: $19.95
ISBN-13: 978-0-936608-40-2
UPC: 0-66066-00056-9

COLOR GUIDE TO STEELHEAD DRIFT FISHING
by Bill Herzog

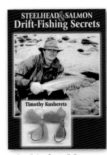

6 x 9 inches, 96 pages.
SB: $16.95
ISBN-13: 978-1-57188-300-1
UPC: 0-81127-00134-7

EGG CURES: Proven Recipes & Techniques
by Scott Haugen
5 1/2 x 8 1/2 inches, 90 pages.
SB: $15.00
ISBN-13: 978-1-57188-238-7
UPC: 0-66066-00492-5

COOKING SALMON & STEELHEAD: Exotic Recipes From Around the World
by Scott & Tiffany Haugen
6 x 9 inches, 184 pages.
Spiral SB: $24.95
ISBN-13: 978-1-57188-291-2
UPC: 0-81127-00120-0

ASK FOR THESE BOOKS AT YOUR LOCAL FLY/TACKLE SHOP OR CALL TOLL-FREE TO ORDER:
1.800.541.9498 (8-5 p.s.t.) • www.amatobooks.com